Beyond
the
Boundaries

A Story of John Baptist de La Salle
Patron of All Teachers

Leo C. Burkhard, FSC

D1414294

New Orleans–Santa Fe Province
De La Salle Christian Brothers
Lafayette, Louisiana

The author wishes to thank the B.C.S. Foundation, Inc.
and Eurofilms for use of still photographs
from the film *Who Are My Own?*

Printed by Saint Mary's Press,
702 Terrace Heights, Winona, MN 55987-1320.

Library of Congress Catalog Card Number 94-71314
ISBN 1-884904-04-1

Beyond the Boundaries

The American actor Mel Ferrer (as seen above) plays the role of
John Baptist de La Salle in the film *Who Are My Own?* based on this story.

To all teachers

and student teachers

whose mission in life

is to touch hearts

Father De La Salle teaching class in Paris.

Proclamation

. . . . "In the fullness of Our apostolic authority, by virtue of this brief and for all time, We constitute and proclaim St. John Baptist de La Salle, Confessor, principal patron before God of all teachers of youth and accord him all the liturgical honors and privileges going with that title.

. . . . Given at Rome, from St. Peter's, and sealed with the Fisherman's ring, the fifteenth day of May, Feast of St. John Baptist de La Salle, in the twelfth year of Our pontificate."

Pope Pius XII

Illustrations

The illustrations are taken from the film *Who Are My Own?* based on the first version of this book entitled *Master of Mischief Makers.* The American actor Mel Ferrer (frontispiece) plays the role of De La Salle and the French actor Marc Michel (cover) impersonates Jacques Delanot. The film won the Special Jury Award of HEMISFILM '68 for its relevance to the Festival theme "Cinema and the Dignity of Man."

1. De La Salle meets Adrian Nyel who asks his help to open a school for poor boys (page 29).

2. De La Salle tries to convince Nyel's disciples to become Brothers. They walk out on him (page 48).

3. De La Salle and two Brothers take over a charity school in Paris to the great dissatisfaction of Monsieur Rafrond (page 60).

4. The King's surgeon, Julien Clément, accuses De La Salle of extorting money from his son to found a training college for teachers (page 155).

5. Sister Louise welcomes Brother François to Parménie (page 172).

6. De La Salle dies in Rouen on Good Friday, April 7, 1719 (page 187).

Acknowledgments

Grateful acknowledgment is extended to:

~~ Brother Joseph Schmidt of Sangre de Cristo Retreat Center, who not only instigated this new edition several years ago as Director of De La Salle Publications, but also collaborated in presenting certain dramatic elements in the text;

~~ Brother Peter Bonventre of Bishop Loughlin Memorial High School in Brooklyn, who untiringly reviewed the text with me over a long period while at the same time offering many a valuable suggestion;

~~ Brother Francis Heuther of Romeoville as copy editor;

~~ Brother Richard Segura, long-time English professor at the College of Santa Fe who taught me to write as a university student and who painstakingly corrected the final manuscript of this new edition;

~~ Brother Donald Mouton who as my student years ago encouraged me to write, then collaborated with me in Europe, and now, as Provincial Superior of the New Orleans–Santa Fe Province, allows me to continue writing and doing historical research on De La Salle;

~~ Mel Ferrer for portraying so fittingly the figure of De La Salle in the film *Who Are My Own?* based on this story;

≈ Marc Michel, the French actor whose picture appears on the cover, for impersonating so naturally the young, enthusiastic, devoted disciple of De La Salle I so wanted to be in the seventeenth century;

≈ the staff of Saint Mary's Press for the artistic presentation of the book.

Introduction

I BELIEVE THAT dreams can come true. Certainly my dreams came true and turned my life into an enchanting adventure.

Let me explain.

The idea of this book was born in Monterrey, Mexico, more than forty years ago. I was a young De La Salle Christian Brother, from the United States, beginning my career as a teacher, and unable at the time to speak Spanish. My situation was enigmatic. Why was I a Christian Brother in the first place? Why had I left home at the age of thirteen to follow this special vocation, knowing all the while that sooner or later I would be asked to make vows that would oblige me to remain a Brother the rest of my life? I felt the urgent need of convincing myself that it would be worthwhile. But how was I to do that? How could I get to know De La Salle, the Founder of the Christian Brothers, well enough to decide once and for all to be one of his disciples forever?

My imagination gave me the answer. In order to meet De La Salle, I would live in seventeenth century France, during the reign of Louis XIV, in the person of young Jacques Delanot, a character I invented for this purpose.

I began to write. My story turned into such a personal and exciting experience that I became identified, as it were, with Jacques Delanot.

Once the manuscript was completed, there remained no doubt at all as to what I should do with my life. I made a final commitment as a Christian Brother in 1947. Students and friends who had been encouraging me and were interested in the manuscript urged me to have it published. The book appeared in 1952, a Grail Publication entitled *Master of Mischief Makers*.

Ten years after writing the story, I was sent to France and given the opportunity of visiting and actually living in many of the places I had known only in imagination. I felt an intimate familiarity with them. Indeed, my youthful dreams of travel and adventure had not only come true, but I was able to verify the authenticity of many happenings that I had described with only an imaginative touch.

If there is one place I remember above all, it is Parménie, a small mountain in the French Alps where the passage of time has left its trace of bloody conquests and of monastic calm, of fabulous legends and of mysterious encounters. There, in the seventeenth century, a saintly peasant woman, a shepherdess of sorts whom the people called Sister Louise, had devoted her life to restoring an old hermitage. And there De La Salle had gone at a particularly dramatic moment in his life. He would probably have remained in this isolated spot till the end of his days had not his disciples discovered his whereabouts and ordered him to return to Paris.

I went there alone one spring morning in 1957. I discovered that the second World War had left the place in total ruins. In 1965, it was my good fortune to be given the task of restoring the hermitage on that mountain top and to live there for more than twenty years.

During my stay there, I had the soul-moving experience of reliving scenes from the life of De La Salle as portrayed in the film *Who Are My Own?* based on the book I had written years before and which I had helped adapt to the screen. Playing the role of De La Salle himself, since Mel Ferrer was unable to be present for the filming, I experienced the deep emotions that the Founder of the Christian Brothers must have felt at that decisive moment in his career. On my desk today, a special jury award, presented to me by the Directors of "Hemisfilm '68" for the film's relevance to the festival theme "Cinema and the Dignity of Man" still reminds me of those moving moments. Scenes from the film serve as illustrations for this book.

The story I am about to tell is then the story of my life as I lived it in the France of De La Salle's time.

This book is a total revision of the earlier one. That is why I have changed its title. Writing it has been a labor of love, challenging me to draw upon my deeper knowledge of the life of John Baptist de La Salle.

Leo C. Burkhard, FSC
Denver, Colorado
Thanksgiving Day
November 1992

1

IN 1672, PARIS could count me, Jacques Delanot, among the hundreds of carefree teenagers who loitered aimlessly in her streets. Cobbled, dirty streets they were for the most part, winding this way and that, in labyrinthine style. They were dark streets where poverty prevailed, but where now and then a carriage belonging to some wealthy member of the nobility drove past in arrogant fashion as if to insult the likes of us who lived in these humble surroundings.

The nobility were the rich. They owned most of the land, lived in beautiful houses, dressed in fancy clothes and had all they wanted to eat and drink. Most of them cared very little for the poor who were the vast majority in Paris. The luckiest of this vast majority were artisans who had some trade by which to earn a living: cobblers, blacksmiths, stone cutters, or carpenters. Many others went outside the city early every morning with their carts to bring in fruit and vegetables to sell in the public market. These, at least, always had something to eat. But there were many others who had nothing at all. They very often became beggars or thieves, or they died of hunger.

The men in the family often went off to fight in the king's armies, leaving wives and children to get along all alone. This had happened to my own father. He never came back. My mother died shortly afterwards, when I was only ten. That's how I came to be staying with an uncle of mine, a blacksmith, in one of the poorest parts of the city, not far from the Church of Saint Sulpice. I liked this old man although he made me work hard.

We lived on Princess Street, a strange name indeed for a street like ours. Down toward the public square and not far from my uncle's shop was a very special building. Outwardly, it wasn't much different from the others nearby. They all touched each other, their second stories leaning out over the cobbled street in unbalanced fashion. But this building in particular had quite a reputation in the neighborhood. It was the parish school. The cranky old teacher could often be seen in the doorway, with a rod in his hand, shouting at us youngsters in the street.

I went to school there three or four times a week, sometimes in the morning, sometimes in the afternoon, like most of the youngsters in the neighborhood. We learned to read, but only in Latin. There were no schoolbooks in French. Of course, we didn't understand what we were reading, but that didn't seem to matter, just as long as we could help the priest at Mass when we served as altar boys. We learned a little arithmetic but hardly any writing. There was a special school where you could learn to write but it was a pay school and I couldn't go there. The Writing Masters ran it and they were very careful to see that nobody else interfered with their rights. Teaching writing was their livelihood.

The school on Princess Street belonged to the parish of Saint Sulpice and was run by a man named Rafrond. He was fat, ugly, and mean. He sat on a big chair on a wooden platform and called us up to him one by one. He made us repeat the lines in Latin that we were supposed to be able to read. While one boy was with him reciting the lesson, all the others did about anything they wanted. When the noise got too loud, Rafrond would come down off his platform with a whip made out of hickory branches tied together and give the nearest troublemakers a good thrashing.

I contributed my share of trouble, though I was very small for thirteen. Often when I got punished for running around the room, I would think to myself: I don't need this; I'm not coming back! But come back I did for only one reason: a young man from the seminary nearby had started coming to the school once a week to teach us catechism. It wasn't because I liked catechism particularly but rather on account of this new teacher. His name was John Baptist de La Salle. He was from Reims, he told us. The first time he came, I watched him curiously. He said hello to each of us, asked our names, asked about our families. I was bashful when he asked my name and what my parents did. When I told him they were dead, he said:

"I'm very sorry, Jacques. That's a reason for us to be good friends. My mother died last July."

No one had ever said anything so kind to me before. I soon began to look forward to his coming every Saturday. He always had fascinating stories to tell about the Holy Land, about the Jews and Romans, or about Jesus and his apostles. He kept us so interested that we never thought about making trouble as we did with old Rafrond. He would take us to church on occasion and explain the ceremonies that took place there or tell us the stories in the stained glass windows. Sometimes he would just take us to visit interesting places in the city, teaching us all the while how to behave in the streets and how to be nice to people we met. We liked to be with him because he always seemed to take a special interest in each one of us and because we learned so many things from him, things to do and things not to do.

Then, one Saturday he didn't come. Another seminarian came instead. We were sorry about the change and wondered what had happened. I learned later from the sacristan that De La Salle had gone back to Reims. His father too had died. Being the eldest, he was obliged to take over the family affairs and look after his brothers and sisters.

Shortly after this, I decided to quit school and go with my uncle, who was moving to Rouen. I promised to help him, but he thought that I was now old enough to get along by myself and that I should find a job as soon as we reached our destination.

Rouen, everyone said, was a very interesting city. It was where Joan of Arc had been burned at the stake. Our teacher, De La Salle, had told us about her in catechism class and I was anxious to see the very spot where it had all happened. I was glad to be on the way there and to sit in our old horse-drawn cart as it jolted along. With every turn of the wheels, we put Paris further and further behind.

2

IT SEEMED THAT our journey would never come to an end. The road was terribly bumpy. In fact it could hardly be called a road at all. It was rather just a pitted track. Sometimes we stopped for hours. At other times, our pace was so slow that I actually fell asleep without any fear of missing the sights along the way.

Yet, these dreary days of travel were not altogether boring, for my imagination was constantly at work inventing all kinds of adventures that might be awaiting me in Rouen.

Then, too, I was told there were many things to be seen in that old Norman city. I remembered, for example, hearing about its famous bridge of boats across the Seine, the same river that I had seen in Paris near the cathedral. I couldn't wait to see it in Rouen.

Finally, after a last turn in the road, the great city came into view in the valley ahead. The river ran along the far side, and there, sure enough, I could see the bridge—a dark, swaying streak across the water, crowded with peasants and animals and carts on their way to the market. What a thrill it would be to cross it! To look down into the dark, deep water on both sides, to see the women and children clinging to their carts for very fear, and to be jostled about in the excitement. I decided at once that I would go there as soon as possible.

As we came on down into the city, I started to count the church spires that shot up here and there, for I had heard apprentices from Rouen boast of the city's seventy churches and monasteries. The finest of them all had been built by the English, someone had said. They had been masters of the town for a long time in the days of Joan of Arc.

Well, here I was in Rouen, my new home. What a change from Paris! The hills close by seemed to protect the city. The timberbuilt houses had a style all their own, strange and different.

I took leave of my uncle and aunt and set out at once for the market where we had agreed to meet in the evening. I chose the market partly because I was famished and there was no likelier place to find something to eat and partly because somewhere near there Joan of Arc had bravely met her death at the stake.

But just a minute! Joan of Arc could wait. What was this coming down the street? A beautiful horse and a carriage! I had seen few carriages in Paris that could match this one, and the horse too was groomed to perfection. Inside rode a beautiful lady—that is, she might have been beautiful if she had not seemed so arrogant. She spotted me on the street and stared at me so hard and so long that I thought she would never take her eyes off me. I looked down at my tattered waistcoat and knee breeches and then back at her. I shrugged my shoulders and glanced up at the coachman. He caught my eye and waved to me in a friendly manner, lifting his hat jokingly.

My reaction to this must have been amusing, because when I turned around I discovered a young man cleaning his boots in a shop doorway, grinning at me.

"Well, why are you staring at me like that? Who was that?"

"You must be a stranger here not to know Madame Maillefer. She's one of the richest people in town. Lives just around the corner. She wouldn't give a penny to a man starving to death, if you want to know."

"Well, I'm going to have a good look anyway. She's beautiful."

"Don't get mixed up with Maillefer!" he said.

"The horse, she's beautiful!"

Judging from the mansion that came into full view as I turned the corner, the Maillefers were really rich. At the gateway, Madame was stepping down from the carriage. Two young lady servants had appeared and were helping her. My eye, however, was on the coachman standing close by, holding the carriage door open. No sooner had the ladies disappeared than he was a different man. He wiped the sweat dripping from his forehead, unbuttoned his jacket, loosened his collar and gave a sigh of relief. Then, patting the mare on the neck, he led her toward the stable at the far end of the yard.

By this time I was close behind the carriage and quite determined to talk to the coachman. He was a bit surprised but not really disturbed at finding me on the premises.

"That is a fine horse you have," I said.

"You bet she is, lad. Where did you come from like that, all of a sudden?"

"I followed your carriage in the street. Who's that lady?"

"Don't you know Madame Maillefer?" Then, in a tone almost as solemn as it was amusing, he added: "Madame Maillefer . . . wife of the Lord Accountant . . . First Lady of this renowned city of Rouen . . . whose humble coachman I am! Antoine Leblanc."

At that, we both laughed. Completely won over by his friendly manner, I questioned him a little further. "She must be very rich. Do you think she would give me a few coins or something to eat, if I asked. I'm half starved!"

"Never!"

"Why not? What's the matter with her?"

"She doesn't know what it is to be kind."

"Is she good to you, at least?"

"Alas, no! She's mean to everyone. I guess it's in her blood. This morning she turned the stable boy out into the street for no reason at all. She has no heart. But I'll do something for you, lad. Come along. What's your name, by the way?"

"Jacques. Jacques Delanot. I just got to Rouen this morning. I came from Paris with my aunt and uncle. They think I should find a job on my own."

"You can just call me Antoine," the coachman said, and he shook hands with me good-naturedly. We went into his room near the stables where he got me something to eat and drink and all the while talked to me about the horses and about his job.

"I see you've taken quite an interest in the lady's horses, Jacques," he said, after a while. "I've got an idea. What would you say about becoming the Lord Keeper of the Stables? That is, if her Highness will have you."

"That would be wonderful."

"I'll handle it for you, young man. Give me a few minutes, will you?"

Antoine left me alone and went in to talk to the lady of the house. When he came out he looked triumphant. He had a suit of clothes thrown over his arm.

"There you are, Jacques. This will be your new uniform," and he added jokingly, "Henceforth, let it be known that Jacques Delanot has become the Lord Keeper and the Lord Sweeper of the Stables, in the service of her Highness, Madame Maillefer!"

I thanked Antoine, who gave me a royal salute to signify my investiture. Then I dashed off in search of my uncle to break the good news.

And so I began my career in Rouen. I worked hard to keep the stables clean, but mostly to keep my job and my little earnings. Every day I learned more about this Madame Maillefer. She lived in luxury if ever a person did. Nothing appeared to be too costly for her table, though the worst sufficed for her servants. The maids, who didn't mind at all talking about their mistress when she wasn't at home, said she attended the late Mass on Sunday just to show off her fancy new clothes.

Disregarding Madame's odd ways, I was more or less content in my little sphere, though I could neither forget nor forgive her unmerciful treatment of the poor who occasionally presented themselves at her door begging for alms. She turned them away with disgust. More than once, on the sly of course, we servants shared our meager rations with these unfortunates.

One day, after I had been stable boy for more than a year and knew pretty well how to cater to the whims of Madame, I was sitting in the shade of a tree near the garden wall when I caught sight of an old crippled beggar about to raise the knocker on the front door. He must not have eaten in days, he looked so weak. How he had approached without my seeing him was a mystery, but there he was in the very act of knocking. It was out of the question to get him away from there now. Yet, I dreaded what I knew for sure was going to happen.

There was something strangely attractive about this beggar. He wasn't just an ordinary tramp. Anyone could see that.

Then it happened. I heard her shrill voice . . . a loud outburst of indignant, abusive language.

"Jacques! Antoine! Come at once and clear this rubbish from my door."

The door slammed. The old man sank to the ground as he tried to move away. It didn't take me long to reach his side and to raise his head. A strange light shone in his deep sunken eyes. Antoine came running and within a few minutes, we managed to get the old man into the stable where we could care for him the best we knew how on my own tattered cot. He wanted only shelter and food. The bowl of soup I brought him renewed his strength a little but we could see that he was far too tired and too sick to live much longer. We stayed near him to the very end. On his wrinkled features, there remained a faint smile of gratitude. He died that night.

I knew I'd be in trouble. The old man had to be buried. Late the next morning, Antoine went to tell the city officials what had happened. I would have to face up to Madame Maillefer alone. When I had worked up enough courage, I went to talk to her. It was the first time I had ever gone to her on my own and my knees trembled.

"Madame," I hesitated, "the old beggar . . . you asked me . . . to take away from your door last evening . . . you see, I took him to the stable. He was so weak . . . he could not walk, Madame . . . he was very ill."

"Chase him out of there! At once! I will have no tramps on the property. Move! Do you hear!"

"But . . . Madame, he's dead!" I waited, holding my breath.

"I'll have no more of this nonsense, Jacques. Get him to move out of there at once!"

"But it's not nonsense, Madame. He is dead and he must be buried. I need something to cover him with."

There was a flare of anger in her eyes. She left the room, mumbling something to herself. When she returned, an old sheet dangled nervously from her hands. She flung it at me contemptuously. It fell to the floor, and before I could reach for it she said:

"He has no right to this, I can assure you. And as for you, Jacques, I'll talk to you later."

When I returned to the stables, I found Antoine there with two grave diggers. We wrapped the body of the beggar in the sheet that Madame had given me and they took him away in their old cart to bury him in the pauper's lot. Although relieved that the burial was taken care of, I still feared the wrath of Madame.

Late that night, in an angry fit, she woke up the whole house and sent one of the servants for me.

"Jacques, I'll have no more of this. I'm going to send for the police to put an end to this nonsense and to bury that scoundrel."

"But, Madame, they buried him yesterday, as you ordered."

"Indeed they did not. Here is the sheet I gave you this very morning. Bury him!"

"Madame, we used that sheet to wrap him in before they took him away. I recall those marks and that torn corner. Please, Madame, ask Antoine and Jeannette."

"Jacques, you are lying. I'll make you pay for this."

"I am not lying, Madame."

"Jeannette," she shouted, "Jeannette, call the servants. All of them."

I watched her growing paler as the moments slipped by. She was trembling with anger by the time the servants had all come in.

"Which one of you put that sheet there!" she asked. "Did you do it, Louise?"

"I assure you, not I Madame. Jeannette and I were in the kitchen when Jacques took it from the floor in the hall where you threw it. We saw him."

"Then who brought it back? Who brought it back?" she squealed.

"Pardon me, Madame." It was Antoine who tried to quiet her. "Jacques brought the sheet to the stable. I helped him wrap the body of the old beggar in it before we buried him."

"Do you mean to say that it came back here all by itself? Or did that filthy beggar bring it here from his grave?"

She seemed terrified. Grabbing her hair in her hands and trembling from head to foot, she whispered in broken tones: "My God, it can't be true!" Then she turned and went madly up the stairs to her room, slamming the door behind her.

I had not been punished. No one had been blamed. In fact, we were all quite satisfied since Madame's disappearance from the scene gave us complete liberty. Jeannette, who had been doing her share of the eavesdropping, whispered it around that Madame had broken down completely and was sobbing uncontrollably.

The following morning, I was surprised to see Madame up much earlier than usual. When I saw her leave the house with one of Jeannette's shawls thrown over her shoulders, I was about to call to her to ask if she wanted the carriage, but Jeannette whispered, "She's walking to church."

"Walking? What does that mean?"

"It means she's lost her mind over that beggar."

3

During the weeks and months that followed the mysterious incident concerning the beggar, a decided change had come over Madame Maillefer. She became very kind to all of us. We got better meals, better clothes and, especially, better wages. And not only us. She never turned another beggar away from her door. She even went out into the city herself to visit the hospitals and orphanages in order to help the sick and the poor.

As for myself, I now had more time to wander about the city and I did so very often. One day I discovered the parish school. Judging from the noise and laughter that came from the open windows, it must have been very much like the school I had attended in Paris under Rafrond. Rouen, I had been told, had more schools than any other city in France.

In mid-winter of the year 1678, of a Sunday morning, I was on an errand of charity for Madame, when I ran across a procession returning to the church. There was quite a large crowd, mostly women and schoolchildren. I stood by, watching curiously, until suddenly a fight broke out among the boys at the end of the line. Within a few minutes, it turned into a real battle. I darted into a nearby shop doorway where I could get my bearings and see what all the commotion was about. I saw two frightened school teachers rush away, trying to protect themselves as best they could. They were now hiding in a passageway down the street. It would take the police to put a stop to this disturbance, I thought.

The procession was about to break up entirely when something strange happened. As if out of nowhere, a small chubby individual wearing a long cloak and a wide-brimmed hat, appeared on the scene. Waving his arms in the air, he headed straight for the center of the battle.

"It's Monsieur Nyel," shouted one of the boys. The name echoed down through the crowd and order was restored as if by magic. The two teachers came back to their posts, wearing an air of shamefaced relief.

I could see this Monsieur Nyel very clearly now. He was an elderly man, probably well past his fifties, short, plump, gray-haired and very affable in manner. My curiosity to find out something more about him would have led me to forget Madame Maillefer's errand altogether, if the group had not at that moment entered the church. I would have to wait for another occasion.

The next day, I went with Madame on another errand, this time to the public hospital. I was agreeably surprised there to meet the principal actor of the previous day's street adventure. Madame introduced me to Nyel but there was no time to talk. He seemed to be a very busy person.

On our way home, Madame told me all about Adrian Nyel. The city officials had put him in charge of teaching the children in the hospital and the orphanage. He had started a small organization of teachers to help him with his work. These men were also sacristans and even practical nurses of a sort. With them, he had set up several charity schools in the city and was acting as a kind of supervisor.

When we had almost reached the house, Madame turned to me again and said in a quiet, almost mysterious way,

"Jacques, I am planning something wonderful with Adrian Nyel. It is still a secret but I shall be able to tell you more about it very soon. You seem to like him already. Perhaps he might like to have your help."

I hadn't much time to think about what she meant, because on arriving home I discovered things in quite a turmoil. Antoine had his carriage drawn up before the side door, and Jeannette and Louise were busy filling it with things belonging to the mistress of the house. Madame had long since sold or given away her rich wardrobe and most of the fine furniture. She seemed bent on ridding herself of everything. The servants said that she was going to sell her residence and live in a much simpler place on the outskirts of the town.

If this were true, then I might soon find myself in a serious predicament. Until now, I had depended entirely on her and what I earned cleaning the stable. I had always been sure of a roof over my head and of food and clothing according to my needs. What was I to expect in the near future? That night I had a talk with Antoine. He told me for certain that Madame was selling her place and with the money she was going to send Nyel to Reims to open a free school for boys. Antoine thought that she would be asking me to go along with him.

This she did before the week was out and though I was wary about getting involved in Nyel's activities, I gladly accepted to go along and help him any way I could. The night before our departure, I found it impossible to sleep. This new venture seemed strange to me and yet I liked the thought of it.

Finally, I dozed off, as tired as if I had already walked the hundred and twenty miles that lay between the cozy little corner in which I slept and Reims, the city of my dreams, where the great Kings of France had been crowned.

4

SPRING WAS IN the air that bright March morning in 1679 when I set out for Reims on foot, in the company of Monsieur Nyel. My youthful ambition and adventurous spirit could scarcely rival his great eagerness to be about this new venture. During the journey, he told me about a priest he had known in Reims, a certain Father Roland, who had founded a society of sisters to take care of orphan girls. Roland had intended to open a school for boys as well, but unfortunately had died before he could complete his plans. All the good work he had done would have died with him if it had not been for another young priest, John Baptist de La Salle, who promised the dying Roland to take care of the orphanage he had founded.

Nyel was surprised when I told him that I knew Father de La Salle.

"He is the very person we're going to see, Jacques. Madame Maillefer is a relative of his. She gave me a letter of introduction for him. We'll look him up later, after we see the Sisters of the Holy Child. He is the kind of person who could help us a great deal in Reims. Besides being very rich, he is a Canon of the cathedral and his family has much influence in the city."

Monsieur Nyel could see that I didn't know what a Canon was.

"Canons are dignitaries who meet in the cathedral several times a day to recite or sing the special prayers of the Church.

They wear a beautiful long cape and robe on these occasions. The bishop has a right to allot certain benefits and church properties to them. That is why Canons have a very comfortable income and are often very rich."

We fell silent as we walked, but my mind was still very much occupied with Father de La Salle. I wondered if he would remember me.

Our journey was long and tiresome. Sometimes we rode in a carriage, but most often we walked from village to village, stopping at inns in the evening to eat and sleep. Now and then some farmer would give us a ride in his cart, but the jolting tired us almost as much as walking.

I liked to listen to the peasants talk about the war with Holland, and sometimes we even met wounded soldiers on their way back home. It seemed as if the king was always fighting wars. Our captains were famous. I often heard the names of Turenne and Condé shouted out in the taverns where we stopped, but conversation about the war seemed to bother Monsieur Nyel. He had his mind on other things.

Well before reaching Reims, I could see the city's great cathedral rising majestically into the clear beautiful sky. Reims had once been the city of the kings of France, but now, in the growing splendor of Louis XIV, its glory had waned and it was at best a merchants' center. Indeed, merchants were everywhere. They were pouring into the cloth market and the wheat market from all directions as we wound our way with them through the narrow streets.

We came to the public square where we could see the cathedral in all its beauty.

"There it is, Jacques, perhaps the most beautiful cathedral in all of France."

I stopped to gaze in wonderment at the magnificent structure where Charles VII had been crowned, but Nyel tugged at my arm impatiently as we continued on our way to the orphanage to meet with the Sisters of the Holy Child.

A timid young Sister opened the convent door and stood back frightened at the sight of us. Our clothes were untidy, travel-stained and dusty.

"Is this the convent of the Holy Child Jesus?" Nyel asked. Then, not waiting for an answer from the little nun, who couldn't seem to recover her composure, he added: "Please tell the Mother Superior that I am here . . . Nyel . . . Monsieur Adrian Nyel from Rouen."

"Yes, Monsieur." Still hesitating, she led us to the parlor, where we waited for a few minutes. Nyel stood near the window turning his big wide-brimmed hat round and round nervously in his hands.

"Good morning, Monsieur Nyel," came a voice from a small woman who had appeared in the doorway on the far side of the room. She seemed full of energy. "I've been expecting you.

Madame Maillefer wrote about your coming. And who is this young man, may I ask?"

I stood up a bit timidly to say hello and then Nyel came to my rescue. "Jacques Delanot, Reverend Mother, one of my helpers."

"That is really wonderful. I know that you have many others in Rouen and that there is no limit to your zeal, but I must tell you beforehand that the difficulties here in Reims may be insurmountable. The city officials do not favor opening new schools."

"Then we must make them favorable. There is no other way."

"It would be very hazardous, especially at this time. You see, Monsieur, the war has been a constant drain on the resources of Reims and the vicinity. The government is determined not to authorize any works of charity that might, in case of public disaster, fall back on it for support."

"But surely they cannot ignore the crying need to take care of the poor children of this city."

"That is true, and I believe your cause is worthy of the great enthusiasm you have for it, Monsieur Nyel. Please do not let me discourage you in any way. But why not consult Father de La Salle? He helped us after the death of Father Roland and he may be able to help you. He happens to be here in the house at this very moment."

She was out of the room even before Nyel had a chance to express his approval. Then her pleasant voice echoed back to the parlor. She had met the priest in the corridor. Nyel moved quickly toward the door.

"Ah, Reverend Father, this is very fortunate. May I present Monsieur Adrian Nyel, a gentleman from Rouen who is interested in founding a school for boys here in Reims. And this is one of his helpers."

I had not taken my eyes off the young priest, having recognized him immediately.

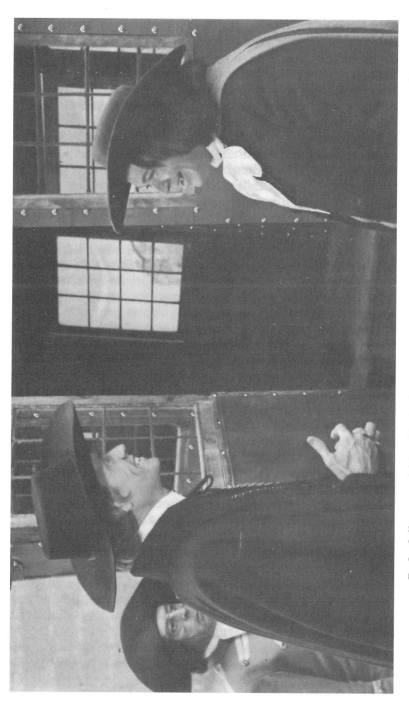

De La Salle meets Adrian Nyel who asks his help to open a school for poor boys.

"It is a pleasure to meet you, Monsieur Nyel. My aunt has written to me about your remarkable achievements in Rouen. And whom do I see here? Jacques Delanot! You were in my catechism class in Paris, weren't you, Jacques? I haven't forgotten your name." He shook my hand in a friendly manner. "It is good to see you again. You have grown up since then. And now, what can I do for you, Monsieur Nyel?"

"I have a letter of introduction from your aunt, Madame Maillefer. It is her desire that I set up a school for boys here in Reims. She has promised financial support."

"That is a serious undertaking. If the project became known publicly, it would meet with great opposition."

"I am not afraid of opposition, Father. Only I need someone influential to back up this project."

"Yes, I understand perfectly well, but to make a stir about it now, without due preparation, would probably ruin its chance to succeed. I suggest that you come to my home for a few days. Your presence there will arouse no suspicion, and I'll see what I can possibly do to help you."

Monsieur Nyel readily accepted the hospitality so generously offered. By evening of that first day, we were comfortably installed in Father de La Salle's home and had met his two brothers, Jean-Louis and Pierre, the only members of his family who were still living with him. I liked them both from the very beginning, especially Jean-Louis, who was fifteen and who looked and acted very much like his older brother. Pierre was a quiet timid lad of thirteen.

The following morning when Monsieur Nyel and Father de La Salle met to discuss their business, I had a chance to talk with Jean-Louis. I admit that I was curious to know more about his older brother.

"It was kind of your brother to let us stay here," I said.

"Oh, he is always doing things like that. Our house is almost a hotel. My brother has many friends among the clergy who always stay here when they come to Reims. My father's friends still come, too, even though he has been dead a number of years. Everyone likes Jean-Baptiste; he has a way with people."

"Is he the oldest in the family?"

"Yes. He was born in 1651."

That made Father de La Salle twenty-eight.

"I was in his catechism class in Paris when he was at the seminary," I said.

"I know he was happy at Saint Sulpice, but he had to come back and take charge when our father died. Jean-Baptiste was ordained just last year."

Jean-Louis paused. "Can you believe that we were eleven children? It's sad to think that four of my brothers and sisters died when they were very young. I'm eighth down the line. After Jean-Baptiste, there is Marie. She got married a few weeks ago to Jean Maillefer—but no relation to the Maillefer you worked for in Rouen." She lives here in the city and has taken my youngest brother, Jean-Remy—he's nine years old—to live with her."

In the days that followed, I learned that Rose-Marie was in a convent in Reims and Jacques-Joseph was in the seminary in Paris. Finally there was Pierre. Indeed, a big family! With both parents dead, Father de La Salle had the heavy responsibility for most of these younger brothers and sisters.

Despite his obligations as a Canon of the Cathedral and his duties as father of the family, Father de La Salle devoted much time to Monsieur Nyel those first weeks.

Eager to resolve things as quickly as possible, he found a priest in the city who was interested in Nyel's project. His name was Father Dorigny. He offered Nyel a house near the church of Saint Maurice to serve as a school. Nyel and I, as well as two young men whom Nyel recruited in the market place, went to lodge with Father Dorigny.

The school opened and dozens of children from the neighborhood began to attend classes. There was no doubt that Nyel had talent. The venture succeeded immediately. Parents spread the good news to other parts of the city and, before five months had passed, Nyel was planning to open a second school. A lady from the parish of Saint James, Madame de Croyère, had offered money for this foundation.

Monsieur Nyel took the matter to Father de La Salle, who listened to him patiently, admiring his zeal but remaining reluctant to approve this new project so soon after the opening of the first school. Father de La Salle clearly preferred seeing one school firmly established and prosperous rather than several poorly organized. Although Nyel had supposedly found two men willing to teach in the school, Father de La Salle still hesitated, asking for time to examine the project. He wanted to be better informed, to seek advice and to meet Madame de Croyère in person.

He was surprised and pleased shortly afterwards to discover how generous and well-disposed this lady was. She had already obtained the approval of the parish priest. Father de La Salle had only to convince Father Dorigny to lodge the newcomers. He did this willingly and promised to help financially. Thus Monsieur Nyel opened his second school in Reims.

Though Father de La Salle was not directly responsible for the foundation of the schools, and had no hand at all in their management, he occasionally dropped in to visit us and to talk to the youngsters in class or to teach catechism. They liked him very much. Sometimes a group of them, poorly clothed and dirty for the most part, would follow him in the street. This created quite a sensation, especially if he happened to meet some of his friends or relatives. They criticized him severely for giving so much of his time and attention to the likes of us.

My thoughts often turned to him during those first months in Reims. I tried to piece together all that I had heard about him. It was rumored that the archbishop had particular plans for him, some important post in the diocese, but that Father de La Salle had refused. He wanted only to be a simple priest in some poor parish. I heard, too, that he had tried to resign as Canon of the cathedral, but this time it was the archbishop who had refused.

Early during the first winter I spent in Reims, an incident occurred which nearly cost Father de La Salle his life. It happened one evening when Father Dorigny, Monsieur Nyel, the other teachers, and I met to discuss what could be done about our living quarters, which had become entirely inadequate. We were waiting for Father de La Salle to arrive to offer his advice. I was convinced that he would find a solution to our problem.

The weather had turned bitterly cold and it had begun to snow. As the hours passed, the storm got worse. Father de La Salle did not arrive and we were getting uneasy. Finally Nyel decided to send me to the De La Salle home to inquire about the priest.

By this time, the snow storm had turned into a blizzard and only with great difficulty did I get across town to Father de La Salle's house. Jean-Louis and his younger brother Pierre told me that Jean-Baptiste had left early that morning on horseback to make a sick call in the country. He should have returned hours ago.

The two boys were frightened and uneasy. Pierre was convinced that his brother had fallen into the hands of robbers and might even be dead. Such things did happen on the outskirts of the city and even more frequently so during the winter months.

I was going to try to make it back to Nyel's meeting to tell the teachers we should search for Father de La Salle, when Pierre heard the sound of horse's hoofs in the courtyard.

Father de La Salle had returned but neither the horse nor the rider had enough strength to go any further. We got him into the house. His face was deathly pale, his hands half frozen. Jean-Louis gave him a hot drink and he lay quietly on the couch by the fireplace.

We couldn't get him to tell us what had happened. He remained strangely silent for a long while. All he finally said was that God had kept him from a terrible death in the snow and cold.

Later, I learned that he had lost his way because of the heavy snowfall and had fallen into a deep gully. He had tried for hours to climb out and get the horse out, but each time he had failed, until finally he was completely exhausted. If he had passed the night there, he would certainly have frozen to death.

I never did get a satisfactory explanation of the whole incident. Neither did his two brothers, who stayed near him the rest of the night and took close care of him for several weeks afterwards. I did hear Father de La Salle refer to this episode years later as one of those moments in life when Providence intervenes in an almost tangible way.

His exposure to the cold and snow that night left him with a kind of rheumatism that was going to cause him great suffering the rest of his life.

5

Ever since that awful night, I noticed a change in Father de La Salle. There was something about him that I had not seen before. Perhaps it was a greater and more personal interest in Nyel and the teachers. I could not exactly say.

The proof of it came one evening when Monsieur Nyel told me that Father de La Salle had rented a house for us very near to his own and that we would move there soon. This would settle our lodging problem. It showed us at the same time how deeply attached he was to our work despite growing criticism on the part of his family and relations.

On Christmas day, 1679, we moved into the new residence, a real palace compared to our former living quarters.

Within a month's time, Nyel recruited two new teachers and opened another school in our very home. It quickly became the most important of the three schools now functioning in Reims. What was still better, at least from our viewpoint, was the new arrangement concerning our meals. At Father Dorigny's there had hardly been enough food for all of us. We were always hungry. Now, since we were living so near Father de La Salle's house, he had his servants prepare meals for us in his own kitchen. One of my jobs was to bring the food over to our house. I'm quite sure that several of Nyel's new school teachers joined our ranks for no other reason than to make sure they would have a place to stay, a bit of money, and good meals.

Nyel knew that in the long run these young men would need a better reason than that to stay with us. He saw the need of motivating us and training us as teachers, of getting all of us to lead an orderly and regular life and of inspiring us with noble ideals. But he didn't feel capable of doing that himself. He was talented as far as organizing the schools was concerned, but he couldn't really manage the teachers as a group. He left us much to ourselves and was often absent from the house or even from the city. He was constantly attracted by new projects.

It became evident that some of the problems we were having with the students and in getting along with one another were getting worse. Some of the teachers were very discouraged, and even three meals and a good house were not going to keep them.

Father de La Salle saw the need for some changes. He had allowed himself to get involved with Monsieur Nyel in this business of schools, almost against his better judgment and only through charity, but he could hardly back out now.

During that first year in Reims, I had turned twenty and found myself too, more than I could even believe, involved in Nyel's undertakings. Not that I particularly wanted to be a teacher, but I liked to be with Nyel and with the youngsters, to bring them bread from Father de La Salle's kitchen and to listen to their stories. Nyel had taught me to read and write and whatever else he could—some arithmetic, history, and geography. I was happy in my own way and glad to be of help.

Monsieur Nyel, however, was restless. He wanted to be on the move again. A request came from Guise, a little town north of Reims where the city magistrates wanted to open a school for the poor. They had heard of Nyel's success with the three schools in Reims. This new possibility gave rise to considerable discussion one night when Father de La Salle happened to be at the house.

The town of Guise was near the sanctuary of Our Lady of Liesse, a place of pilgrimage for many people in the surrounding area. Monsieur Nyel used this argument to favor his new project, knowing that Father de La Salle often went there himself through devotion to the Blessed Mother.

Despite this attraction, Father de La Salle opposed the move. He felt that the work in Reims was still insecure and would come to ruin if Monsieur Nyel were to absent himself for any length of time. He spoke to us very frankly but Nyel would not be persuaded. As for the teachers, their opinion was divided. Some, still craving adventure, sided with Nyel. Others wanted to consolidate the work at home.

Nyel finally decided to make the trip during Easter week that year, 1680. He asked me to accompany him. This was going to be the last trip I would make with Adrian Nyel. He accomplished nothing during the ten days we were away. He admitted that he had made a serious mistake in not listening to Father de La Salle. We returned, crestfallen, and unhappy, to Reims, but none of the teachers were at home to welcome us back. Fearing that they might have just given up and walked off, we hurried to find Father de La Salle. As we approached his house, we could hear music coming from the front room. I remembered that his sister, Marie, played the harpsichord and that she sometimes used her brother's home to entertain her friends because she was very fond of the spacious ballroom.

We knocked. One of the servants came to let us in. The music stopped. The group around the harpsichord was evidently disturbed by our unexpected appearance. Marie rose from her place, rearranged the music that had fallen to the floor, and came toward Monsieur Nyel, who seemed even more embarrassed than she.

"Good afternoon, Madame," he said nervously. "I am very sorry to have interrupted your concert. Please excuse me. I am looking for your brother, Jean-Baptiste. Do you know where he is?"

"In the garden with your teachers. I dislike calling them teachers, they are so uncouth. However, I am glad, Monsieur Nyel, that you have returned to Reims. Some of my friends said that you had no intention of coming back and that Jean-Baptiste would be obliged to replace you. In fact, he seems to have done so already, judging from what I have seen here this past week."

"Do you really think so? It would be a great blessing for the schools."

"Indeed not! Our uncle and the Archbishop will see to that. There is still time to put a stop to this foolishness. I will show you to the garden if you wish, Monsieur."

We followed her into the courtyard. The teachers were there, gathered around Father de La Salle, listening attentively. Marie then turned abruptly and walked back into the house without another word. I saw clearly that trouble was brewing in the De La Salle family because of us.

While Monsieur Nyel and I had been absent in Guise, the teachers had spent much of their time with Father de La Salle, at his home, discussing school problems. They had even made a kind of spiritual retreat together. All this was new to them but they seemed to like it. As for Monsieur Nyel, he was overjoyed.

"Just think, Jacques," he told me a few days later, "in the space of ten days, Father de La Salle completely transformed the teachers. They now go about their teaching in a new inspired way. I have asked him to take complete charge of them. He is hesitating still but if he accepts, then I shall be free to set up schools in Laon, Guise, Chartres, Paris—everywhere, Jacques, everywhere! Do you see what this means to me?"

While Monsieur Nyel waited impatiently for an answer, Father de La Salle, strangely enough, disappeared from the scene. The gossip at the church doors on a Sunday morning was that he had finally come to his senses and had abandoned the whole affair. In his absence, Marie had not allowed the teachers to come to his house at all.

The truth of the matter was, however, that Father de La Salle had merely gone to Paris to consult Father Barré, a saintly old priest who had himself at one time tried to start schools for poor children. When Father de La Salle finally returned to Reims, he not only continued to help the teachers, but he took them into his own home for good, to live with him.

News that certain scruffy individuals were living in the De La Salle house shook the neighborhood. When De La Salle's uncle learned what his nephew had done, he was outraged. Although other relatives and friends protested publicly, Father de La Salle seemed to pay little attention to the criticism. His sister Marie came angrily one day to take her younger brother Pierre away with her. She and her uncle were among the loudest in protesting the turn events had taken. I rejoiced to see that Jean-Louis remained faithful to his brother. He would leave, too, eventually, but to enter the seminary. I might never have known just how much Father de La Salle's devotion to our cause was costing him had I not stumbled on something that left a deep impression on me.

I was returning from an errand one night and had to pass near the church of St. Remigius. It was dangerous for any of us to be on the streets at night, especially alone, but on this particular occasion there had been an urgent need. As I passed the church, I thought of spending a minute or two there. On the steps I met François, the sacristan, making ready to lock up.

"Good evening, François. Could you let me go in for a few minutes?"

"Sorry, Jacques, but it's too late. I've got to lock up and be going."

There was an air of nervousness about François tonight. I could detect it in the tone of his voice and in the manner in which he tossed the ring of keys back and forth from hand to hand. I wondered if something in the church had given him a scare.

"I'll only be a minute. Say, what's the matter with you tonight, François?"

"Nothing. I'm just in a hurry. That's all."

"I thought for a while that St. Remigius had turned over in his grave or was night-walking in the nave. Can't you let me go in for a minute or two?"

"You win, Jacques," he said at last, "but promise not to make a sound."

The door slid quietly open and I slipped inside in an instant. The glowing sanctuary lamp cast its blood-red light upon the altar. Here and there, some faint glimmer reflected on the pillars in the nave. To the left, I could see another light, that of a vigil lamp perhaps, coming from a side chapel—the very chapel, in fact, where the tomb of St. Remigius was located. Yes, François had shown it to me before. I remembered now.

Something urged me to go in that direction.

The pillars concealed me from view and, as I neared the side chapel, I could make out the figure of someone kneeling there in the dark, silhouetted against the light of a single candle burning before the altar. There was no mistaking that figure; it was Father de La Salle. I watched him for a few moments, surprised and intrigued, as I began to realize, perhaps for the first time, what prayer was all about.

Then I heard his words ever so faintly.

"Lord, it is your loving hand that has led me thus far and has dealt with me in this manner. It tears my heart out to see how my family and friends are opposing the work you have led me to do. I love them and I love the teachers too. Continue to lead me on your paths. I adore now and always, in all things, your holy will in my regard."

It took me but an instant to realize my own position. I felt a deep remorse at having intruded, though unnoticed, on his privacy. At the same time, a gush of admiration for him filled my whole being. Here was the man I must look up to and follow through thick and thin, as courageously as I could. Deep in my heart I pledged to do it.

François was waiting for me outside. He slipped the key into place and turned it slowly. When I looked at him as much as to say: "Do you know, too?" he pulled the key out of the lock and shrugged his shoulders.

"It's a little agreement we have, Jacques," he said, starting down the steps. "I could never find out why he spends the night there, especially in that chapel, but he often does. Figure it out for yourself, if you can. Good night."

In a moment, François disappeared into the darkness that had now settled over the city. I stood there alone.

That night, I had met Father de La Salle on altogether new ground, and the meeting had given me a spark of faith that I felt could never be extinguished this side of heaven.

6

WE WERE WALKING toward the outskirts of the town, Father de La Salle and I. Behind us, the din and bustle of the market place could hardly be heard. We entered the quiet quarter of St. Remigius. I could see the spires of the church dedicated to this great saint of France towering above the houses on the left. Asleep there in his tomb, St. Remingius may have been aware of my presence in the church that night several months ago, but I felt sure that Father de La Salle had never known. I still felt the strong impact of that experience, and I had returned to pray there on several occasions.

Things were becoming clearer to me now that I had pledged in my heart to remain faithful to Father de La Salle, no matter what might happen.

Things were changing for another reason too. Some of the teachers had tired of their work and no longer liked the demands put on them by Nyel and Father de La Salle. The life of a teacher had been attractive at first, but they had never expected to live a disciplined life as they now did under the guidance of Father de La Salle. Some of them abandoned the group and left the house without giving any notice whatever. Others gradually became discouraged and asked to leave. At one time, there remained two teachers to look after the three schools in the city. There seemed little hope that the schools would survive. Monsieur Nyel took some classes himself and, for the first time, asked me to lend a hand. I was happy to do it, especially since Jean-Louis de La Salle had volunteered his services too. Then, when the future looked darkest, new young men asked to join us and the regular routine of classes resumed in all the schools.

Father de La Salle and I walked on silently. It is hard to say where my wandering thoughts would have carried me if Father de La Salle had not finally broken the silence when we reached New Street.

"There, Jacques, just what I have been looking for," he said as we turned in the direction of a large, plain house to our right.

"We shall be moving again soon, that is, if Providence has really destined this place to be our new home. I have been told that it is available for renting."

The house in question was a spacious building with a fine garden. It seemed well suited to house the teachers. I liked the prospect of moving here with Father de La Salle. Life in his home on St. Margaret Street had become very painful to all of us because of the frequent intrusion of his family and friends into our affairs.

However, I had a problem on my mind which I found hard to submit to him. It was about this question of Providence. It had been bothering me for a long time. Monsieur Nyel had tried to explain it all to me but I still didn't quite understand. He had told me that Providence was the loving care that God takes of his creatures. It was the way God arranges events in our lives for our own good even though we don't always see it his way. Looking back on my own life, I could already recognize that someone was really looking after me. It was strange, to say the least, how I had met Jean-Baptiste de La Salle in Paris, and then Madame Maillefer in Rouen, and how she had introduced me to Monsieur Nyel. He, in turn, had led me back to Father de La Salle. Was Providence really behind all this?

I had heard Nyel's helpers, too, talking about Providence. For them, it consisted in having enough to eat and drink and a comfortable place to sleep. Their point of view had nothing to do with God's care; it did not at all agree with Father de La Salle's way of thinking. That is what bothered me most. How could I tell him? Would he understand?

I had waited in the garden while he had gone in to discuss his business with the proprietors of the house. When he came out, I could see that he was pleased.

"Everything is fine, Jacques. We shall be able to move here very soon now. God is good to us."

"Father de La Salle, didn't you say that we would move if Providence had really destined this home for us? In fact, you often talk to us about Providence. You tell the teachers to trust in Providence. Do you know what they say?"

"No, Jacques, but the other day I read you that beautiful passage in the Gospel where Jesus talks about how our heavenly Father takes care of the birds of the air and the flowers of the field. And how Providence clothes the lilies of the field and makes them more beautiful than even King Solomon in all his glory. I am amazed at the care he takes of us."

"The teachers and I talked for a long time after you left about this idea of Providence," I said, "they just don't agree with you, especially Nicolas Vuyart, and he has lots of influence with the others. He says it's easy for you to trust in Providence because you're rich, but what about us?"

Father de La Salle stopped abruptly. He looked sad and pensive.

"You are right to question me, Jacques," he said, and Vuyart is right too. In fact, I have been asking myself a lot of questions ever since I got involved with Monsieur Nyel and the schools. I am well aware of the gap that separates us. That is why I am going to move away from my home and my family and live with you. I think God wants me to do that. As for my canonry, it has already become an obstacle between us. I can't honestly be a good Canon and at the same time devote my life to work in the schools. I believe that I shall have to give it up too. We shall be coming to the Church of Saint Remigius in a few minutes. Let's stop there, Jacques. I need some time to think and pray about what you just said."

This time the church was not dark. Multi-colored light streamed in through huge stained glass windows depicting great figures of the Church of France. In one I saw Clovis, the King, being baptized by Saint Remigius. In another, Jesus sat in the midst of a group of children on some Palestinian hillside. I couldn't help but recall how, in a classroom on Princess Street in Paris, a group of poorly clad youngsters had listened to a young seminarian just as attentively as these stained glass figures in the window listened to Jesus. And there, a few yards in front of me, knelt that same figure, absorbed in prayer. It was only weeks afterwards that I knew about the momentous decisions being formulated deep in his soul at that very moment.

"You know, Jacques," he said as we left the church, "Monsieur Vuyart is quite right. It is hard for a rich person to have real trust in Providence. The poor have by far the greater advantage."

We reached the De La Salle house on Saint Margaret Street a little before the teachers returned from the schools. Nyel was absent again, having gone to Rethel, a small town not far from Guise, to make arrangements for a school there. That evening Father de La Salle broke the surprising news. He was going to give up his home. As he talked, my imagination wandered back to the day when Nyel and I first set foot in this very mansion. How things had changed! Father de La Salle, who had taken us so generously into his own home, was now giving up that home which contained so many of his most cherished memories. To leave it for good and to live with us would put a very definite barrier between him, his brothers and sisters, and all his relatives. It would identify him forever with the work of the schools.

By the end of the week, Father de La Salle and all of us had moved to the house on New Street. Tongues started wagging again and objections from his relatives and friends rang out from every quarter. To add to the confusion, news spread rapidly that Father de La Salle had also decided to resign his position as Canon of the cathedral. As far as his relatives were concerned, this was nothing less than insanity. The Archbishop, however, approved the decision and, before anyone could formally object, the papers were signed. Only when Father de La Salle returned to our house on New Street that evening with these official papers in hand, were we convinced that he had thrown in his lot totally with us. He seemed as jubilant at having given away this position of honor and financial security as any ordinary person would have been to receive a great legacy. We were happy to know that he was completely on our side but we began to ask ourselves what he would do next.

Some of his relatives must have been asking questions too, because the very next day while I was busy cleaning the front part of the house, one of his uncles called at our new home. I overheard the entire conversation.

"Well, well, how is my little fool today?"

"Quite well," came De La Salle's unperturbed reply. "And yourself? Won't you be seated?"

"Well, I hardly know if I may. I don't feel at home in this strange place. Have you sold the family home? Am I too late to claim some pieces of furniture that I lent your father?"

"No, you are in time, Uncle."

"Now, listen to me. What is this I hear about resigning your canonry? Are you mad or do my ears deceive me?"

"I am not mad, to my knowledge, Uncle, and neither do your ears deceive you. I resigned a week ago, and my resignation was accepted by the Archbishop."

"So I cannot stop you. You are of age and are supposed to be sane. But how will this foolish conduct of yours affect your brothers and sisters?"

"They will be well provided for. Don't worry."

"You resigned in favor of your brother Jean-Louis, I hope."

"No, I chose Father Faubert. He is a pious and zealous priest and he is in great need."

"What! You preferred him to your own brother? You surely know that Faubert is of very humble origin. He is not worthy of such a promotion."

"I prefer to let another set the boundaries of worthiness, or unworthiness, Uncle. I hope to have done the will of God."

"The will of God! The will of God! Is it the will of God to ruin the reputation of your family, to give up your home, to forfeit your career and destroy the name of De La Salle? It was bad enough to associate with those uncouth characters in the first place, but to share the family home with them and then leave your own home and move into this house with them and now to resign your canonry to accommodate them! You've resigned your future, Jean-Baptiste, you're ruined. You could have made something of yourself. You were destined to be a Bishop. Now you're nothing! You've cut yourself off from the wealth of the family and from a high position in the Church."

"My wealth, my dear Uncle, consists in being rich enough to be free to do what God asks of me, to help people live beyond the boundaries that enslave them, their poverty, their riches, their ignorance, their fear, their blindness."

"What are you talking about? Stop this nonsense!"

"I've decided to throw my lot in with these uncouth characters, as you call them, and try to educate the children of the poor, to open their minds and let the sun shine in."

"You've gone mad, Jean-Baptiste. You've become a revolutionary!"

"I hope not, Uncle, because the teachers and the children need my help and I hope to give it to them."

Then I suppose you are crazy enough to waste your inheritance to finance this stupid venture?"

"Well, maybe even more crazy than that. We'll see, my dear Uncle. Maybe I'll just give everything away and rely totally on Providence."

"This doesn't make any sense at all! What about your family, your future, and all that you have here?"

"Uncle, I don't want to be possessed by possessions. Providence has led me this far and I intend to let Providence lead me even further."

"You are a dreamer, Jean-Baptiste, a foolish conceited dreamer. I hope that before you take yourself to the poorhouse, you will come to your senses."

I listened to the heavy footsteps leaving the study and felt a strange foreboding rising within me. If Father de La Salle were to carry through on his idea of giving away everything he owned, then where would the teachers be? What would become of the poor children in our schools? We needed the support of his money.

Monsieur Nyel had fifteen teachers now, or so they called themselves, but they were poor, poorly educated, poorly clothed, poorly disciplined and had no financial security. Nyel had found them loitering in the market place and had given them a minimum amount of training. With his help, it is true, they had succeeded in opening schools in several nearby towns: Laon, Guise, and Rethel. He was acting as supervisor of these, but I had seen little or nothing of him in Reims during the past several months.

Free now of his duties as Canon and separated from his family, Father de La Salle began to devote more and more of his time to helping the teachers. He taught them to employ their time well and he assisted them in preparing their classes. This produced excellent results. The popularity of the schools did not go unobserved by Father de La Salle's relatives, who saw him drifting farther and farther away from their style of life. While petty wars were going on between them as to how they should react to Father de La Salle's behavior, there were greater and far more serious troubles facing France. The King's troops were meeting with defeat and the demand for food and clothing for the army increased day by day.

By autumn of that year, 1684, conditions in Reims were getting worse. Then news began flowing that all was not well in the provinces. The crops had failed miserably and everything pointed to a hard winter ahead. Doubtless some of the teachers were with us just to be sure of a roof over their heads and three good meals. Beggars called at the door every day and Father de La Salle would never allow them to be turned away hungry.

As winter drew near, the number of unfortunates increased. The workhouses were full to overflowing and policemen were posted everywhere to keep the needy from breaking into shops. These were unmistakable signs of what was yet to come.

Famine more severe than the poor peasants of the northern provinces had seen in years settled upon the area. Reims looked more like a hospital than a city; the sick and the dying were everywhere. Poor, homeless outcasts of society, streaming in from the surrounding area, roamed the streets, scantily clad, in search of whatever could satisfy their hunger, completely disregarding cleanliness and the risk of contagion. Despite the police, thieves broke into shops in search of food but more frequently than not came away empty-handed. Hundreds died in the streets of cold and starvation.

Threatened by this same prospect, Monsieur Nyel and the teachers from the outlying towns returned to Reims to live with us again. There was work for everyone. If not busy in the classroom, we spent our time distributing bread to hundreds of starving children. The three schools in the city were overcrowded. Most of the boys came more to satisfy their hunger than to seek instruction. It was a touching scene to see some of them hide the bread in their ragged clothes and carry it off to share with their hungry parents.

Few among the rich ventured from their homes for fear of disease or robbery, but Father de La Salle thought nothing of going into the city to help those in need. He dipped into the reserves of his own money to buy bread and other supplies. He had food sent to the schools where all of us helped distribute it to the poor. In his generosity, he cared for all who came begging, even though they had no connection with the schools. There were many, too, among his former friends who were suffering but who were ashamed to present themselves. He sought them out and had me take food to them privately, so as not to wound their feelings. More than once I was robbed before I reached my destination. Then Father de La Salle would say, "That's all right, Jacques. Those who took the food probably needed it even more than our friends."

That sad winter passed and spring came. The land still failed to produce the wheat needed for bread, and there were still hungry mouths to feed. Even the greatest fortune would have been quickly exhausted with so many to care for over such a period of time. We knew only too well that one day Father de La Salle's fortune would give out. When he could no longer care for those who came to the schools, he took a basket himself and went begging in the streets or at the homes of the wealthy. Some former friends turned him away in scorn, but others, forced to admire his courage and generosity, gave him what he needed.

The reaction of the teachers was very different. I remember being with them one night at the supper table. We had nothing at all to eat, not even a small piece of black bread to share. I had gone begging with one of them that afternoon, but we had both returned empty handed.

"Where is Father de La Salle?" I asked, "and Monsieur Nyel?"

"Your Monsieur Nyel has rich friends with whom he can eat, drink and make merry," Vuyart said bitterly. "As for Monsieur de La Salle, he is off begging again, I presume. He should have kept his money in the first place. We wouldn't be in a fix like this if he had been reasonable. Maybe he won't come back at all. He has no obligations to any of us. He can close the schools any day. Then we'd be in the streets as before.

"He'd never do that, Nicolas." I said. "We all know better."

Then all of a sudden, we heard footsteps and Father de La Salle appeared in the doorway opening into the hall.

"No," he said, "I'll never close the schools, even though I'm not the one who opened them."

"Then, what'll we do?" Vuyart retorted. "We can't live like this. What'll we eat? You gave our food to beggars in the street! We came here to be teachers, not martyrs!"

Then turning toward all of us at the table, Vuyart shouted angrily: "Why don't you speak up, the rest of you? You're a bunch of hypocrites! When he's not here, you're free enough with your tongues!"

One of the teachers stood up. It was Fernand Lagrange, the youngest of the group and a friend of Vuyart. He was nervous and angry.

"I'm with you, Vuyart. I'm leaving. We can do better on our own. Come along, Massard, and you, Deville."

One by one, the teachers got to their feet and moved toward Vuyart. I remained seated at the far end of the table.

"We're leaving, Monsieur de La Salle," Vuyart said. "We hope you'll understand. It's not a rebellion. We just don't want to go hungry any longer, that's all. We can't survive on dreams!"

"I understand," Father de La Salle answered very quietly. "I would like to offer you more, but I have nothing left to share with you, unless it's that dream I have, as you say, of being poor

De La Salle tries to convince Nyel's disciples to become brothers. They walk out on him.

and of devoting my life to the poor children who come to our schools. If you want to come back some day, you'll be welcome. Thank you for your sincerity and the help you've given Monsieur Nyel and me up to now. I think he'll understand, too. I hope we meet again soon."

Slowly all the teachers followed Vuyart to the door, almost sheepishly, I thought. Then they were gone.

Night had fallen over Reims.

The two dying candles on the table, amidst the empty places, spoke to me more eloquently than any person could have at that moment. Father de La Salle had taken his place at the other end of the table and had buried his head in his hands.

I had seen him like this once before, that unforgettable night in the Church of Saint Remigius. The pledge I had taken then, to be faithful to him, came back very vividly to my mind. Here we were again, the two of us, alone. The silence was frightening. One of the candles burned itself out just as the midnight hour sounded from the church tower. In the semidarkness, Father de La Salle looked up.

"It's kind of you to have stayed on, Jacques. But you had better go like the others. I can't care for you any longer. You've been wonderful in helping Monsieur Nyel and me, but that, it seems, was all a dream. Real life is more difficult and one must face it all the same."

"I won't leave you, no matter what happens. Maybe some of the teachers will come back. And if they don't, we'll find others. I want to be with you. I can teach now, I'm sure of it. Monsieur Nyel prepared me. We'll start all over again. I have some friends who want to help. They were in school with your brother Jean-Louis before he went to the seminary. I'll get them to come, if you'll let me. And Monsieur Nyel is sure to come back."

"Thank you, Jacques. I've been wanting all along to ask you to be a teacher. I'm sure you'll make a good one."

He stood up and came toward me with open arms. He hugged me affectionately and then, standing, with his hands still on my shoulders, he said, "Yes, we'll start again, and the house we're going to build will be the Lord's house, founded on Providence alone, and it will not crumble if we trust in him, regardless of the winds and storms."

THE MONTH OF May came to the Reims, bringing with it all the beauty that only spring can bring to the meadows and hillsides of France. Along with the promise of a golden harvest, it brought new life and hope to hundreds of peasants. It brought victory to our soldiers on the battlefield. It brought even more than all this, a little procession of black-robed figures—thirteen of them—to the famous sanctuary of Our Lady of Liesse. And I was one of those thirteen, the first Brothers of the Christian Schools. We had walked almost all night from Reims to this little village not far from Laon, a distance of about thirty miles.

So many things had happened since that memorable day when the teachers had abandoned Father de La Salle. Jean-Louis's two friends had come to replace those who had deserted. It was the first time that young men with some schooling had come to join our ranks. They gave up their fine homes, their money, and their promising future to share Father de La Salle's poverty and to become humble school teachers. They were soon his most fervent disciples.

Then Monsieur Nyel returned bringing several others. He had even convinced Nicolas Vuyart to come back. I was quite surprised at this because Vuyart had always been the most outspoken and critical whenever difficulties arose, but he was very talented as a teacher. Father de La Salle made no objections and received him as if nothing had ever happened.

We were twelve now as we gathered before the statue of Our Lady. I remember most of their names. Besides Nicolas Vuyart, there were Gabriel Drolin, Jean Lozart, Cosmos Boiserins, Henry L'Heureux, and Jean Patois, whom we called Antoine. Then there was Maurice—I don't remember his last name—and Jean Jacquot, who was the youngest, and Nicolas Bourlette, whom people in Reims called Brother Modestus because of his simplicity, his serenity and his kindness to everyone, especially his pupils.

Brother Jean-François had been the first of Father de La Salle's disciples to die, shortly after we had moved to the house on New Street. Four others followed him to the grave within a brief period: Brother Maurice, Brother Cosmos, Brother Lozart, and Brother Bourlette. This was not really surprising because everyone in our little community tried his best to imitate the example set by Father de La Salle, eating little, living in dire poverty, working long hours and sometimes neglecting rest in order to have more time for prayer. It was a hard life in many ways, but we were happy all the same and proud to be associated with him in this new venture, because we loved him most dearly.

We had agreed to be called Brothers, Brothers of the Christian Schools. There was no mistaking Father de La Salle's purpose now. His own commitment had helped us see a vision of what our life and mission could be. We were the first members of a new religious community and we were to devote our entire lives to teaching the poor. We would not be priests nor would we get married. These were two different ways of life that we gave up so as to devote all our time and energy to work in the classroom. We were to be real educators. This was an entirely new idea among laymen in the Church. The novelty of it all was going to bring us a great deal of opposition and even serious persecution.

Another thing that was going to cause us lots of trouble was the way we now dressed. On Father de La Salle's strong recommendation, we began to wear a simple black robe that reached half way below our knees. It was not at all like the cassock or soutane that priests wore, with a fancy waistband and buttons down the front. He did not want us to be mistaken for priests, and yet it set us aside from people in all other walks of life. With this robe, we wore a white collar with two long bands turned down in front, and a very wide-brimmed hat. Winter had been so cold that he added a kind of cloak to our apparel, one with long dangling sleeves like the one peasants wore, only ours was black and made out of heavy, rough material. Our shoes, too, were heavy and clumsy, like those that ploughmen used in the fields.

At first, people made fun of us in the streets because of this strange attire, but we ignored them and were happy to be like the poor who came to the schools. Our new attire gave us a feeling of community, of fraternity, and of dedication to our special mission.

Father de La Salle also gave us new first names to show that we were now new men and had taken on new responsibilities. I received the name Brother François. We all agreed to make a vow of obedience. We promised to obey Father de La Salle as our superior and to be faithful to the rules and regulations we had drawn up with him, and to teach the poor in whatever school or city he might send us. It was to put a seal, as it were, upon these promises that we had come to the sanctuary of Our Lady of Liesse.

We had come here for another reason, too. Father de La Salle had a very special devotion to Mary, Mother of Jesus. He wanted to place this new society of teachers under her protection. We were to love and respect her and to teach our pupils to love her.

Our Society had been born at a time of national crisis, when the country seemed hopelessly involved in political conflicts, and when famine and disease had sucked the very lifeblood of the nation. Now, here we were, the first Brothers of the Christian Schools, kneeling at the feet of Our Lady, in the very spot where our father and founder had often come to pray in troubled times, and where he had asked Mary to guide him in his new undertaking.

We all knelt around him, with lighted candles in our hands, and pronounced the vow of obedience. Deep in my soul, I thanked God for this call to a community life and I asked the Blessed Mother to be allowed to spend the years that lay before me in the close company of Father de La Salle. Somehow I felt assured that this favor would be granted.

Among ourselves, we talked about going to Paris some day to open schools there too. Then something happened in Reims that affected all of us. Adrian Nyel appeared one day unexpectedly after having been away in Guise and Laon for many months without seeing us. He spent much time alone with Father de La Salle and then told us later in the evening that he had decided to return to Rouen to retire. He considered his task accomplished and wanted to leave Father de La Salle a free hand in the government of the society. He acknowledged very modestly that he had only been an instrument in the hands of Providence and that

Father de La Salle was the real founder of the Society. He expressed a desire to see Brothers in Rouen some day and promised to prepare the way.

We were never to see him again. His health declined very rapidly after he left us and he died a short time afterward. We were all very much moved and saddened by the loss. Father de La Salle celebrated a solemn Mass to honor the memory of this courageous and zealous teacher. All the Brothers and pupils from our schools in Reims took part in the ceremony. It was a great and glowing tribute to Adrian Nyel, whom we all loved.

By this time we numbered more than twenty Brothers working in seven schools in Reims and nearby towns. Father de La Salle had made it his principal concern to mold his little band of followers into a real community. He was the superior from the start. He became our spiritual director by the free and deliberate choice of each of us. This fostered unity among us and we began to make his vision and spirit our own. He in turn sought to win over our hearts and so lead us voluntarily to God. He introduced nothing by sheer authority but rather encouraged us to be creative and to explore new ways of improving our teaching ability and our life in community. In this way we became, as it were, our own legislators.

In 1687, Father de La Salle opened a training college to prepare teachers for rural areas. Not wishing to send Brothers alone into country villages, and yet seeing the great need for teachers there as well, he accepted an opportunity to train a group of young men who had been chosen and sent to him by village priests who admired the effectiveness of our schools. He lodged these future teachers in our house on New Street. They followed our schedule during the time of training but they made no vows and they did not wear the Brother's robe. Neither were they destined to become priests or Brothers, but several of them, attracted by the example of Father de La Salle, actually did become members of our community. Under the expert guidance of Brother Henry L'Heureux they learned the techniques of teaching. They were also taught religion, the reading of manuscripts and printed type, notions of grammar, spelling and composition, letter writing and copying, arithmetic, the system of weights and measures, and plain chant. This last subject was very important because in rural parishes these newly trained teachers would have to direct the singing during church services.

In addition to this training college, Father de La Salle opened another kind of school in our house. We called it a junior

novitiate. It was for boys fourteen or fifteen years old who wanted to become Brothers but who were still too young. Our superi-
or drew up a special program for them and spent much of his
time preparing them to become members of our community.
This experiment not only proved very successful, but it assured a
steady increase in our numbers.

Our community was now very well established in Reims and
we had great hope for the future. Up to this point Father de La
Salle had directed things himself, although he allowed us to participate in drawing up regulations for ourselves and for the
schools. One day, he totally surprised us with an entirely new
idea.

"Brothers," he said, after we had all gathered at our home
on New Street and had spent several days in retreat, "we have a
very important matter to decide. It does not concern the schools
directly. They are functioning very well, thanks to all of you. It
concerns the kind of government that I think our community
should have in order to insure its unity and continuity. You all
remember Monsieur Nyel. He was not a priest and yet it was he
who started this work. I am convinced that it is now time for one
of you to become the superior of our community."

The idea left us dumbfounded. Up till now we had simply
taken it for granted that Father de La Salle, although a priest, was
really one of us and would always be the superior. We did not
know how to respond. Finally, Brother Antoine spoke up. He remembered Father de La Salle as a Canon at the Cathedral and
had served his Mass on many occasions when he was an altar
boy there. He had told me once that it was our superior's example in giving up his canonry and his family fortune that had convinced him to enter our society rather than study for the
priesthood. Antoine and I were good friends and I was anxious to
hear his opinion.

"What will the Archbishop say, Father de La Salle? He will
never allow it. I remember that he was very reluctant to allow
you to resign your canonry."

"This matter does not concern the Archbishop, Brother Antoine. We need not inform him. It will be the Brothers' decision.
You are not dependent on him, except of course, as ordinary
Christians. I am the only one directly subject to his authority because I am a priest. And that is precisely why I think you should
choose a Brother as superior. It will leave you entirely free in the
future to make decisions of your own. Otherwise there will always be conflict of opinion and interference from without."

I understood very well what Father de La salle was trying to say. He had given up his canonry and his connections with the nobility. He had stepped down to our social level to make sure that there would be no class distinction among us. But what would he do now, if we chose a Brother as superior? We had to know.

"Father de La Salle," I asked, "if we elect a Brother as superior, will you stay with us? You have done much more than Monsieur Nyel. You do not have to back away just because he did. You are the real father of this family. We like to call you Father and we always will."

"You are indeed my real family. All of you. That will never change. It is for your own good that I am asking this of you. I am convinced that Providence wants it this way. I will not back away. I will do whatever you ask of me."

We were amazed and deeply moved by this declaration. It left us little choice but to give in to Father de La Salle's request. The election took place on Trinity Sunday. Brother Henry L'Heureux received the majority of the votes and became the superior of the community. He was a wise and prudent man and we loved him, but somehow the situation seemed strange. The fact that we had been asked to keep the election a secret was even more strange. It created a state of uneasiness among us. Father de La Salle alone was satisfied with the new arrangement, going out of his way to show deference and obedience to Brother Henry. He would do nothing without the new superior's permission.

It was his very obedience that betrayed him a short time later and caused us to question the election of Brother L'Heureux. Father de La Salle's sister, Marie, was the first to discover that something unusual had happened at the Brothers' house on New Street. She came to the door one day, all in a flutter, asking for her brother Jean-Baptiste. She was organizing a reception for the Duke of Mazarin, who was a close friend of Father de La Salle and a benefactor of the Brothers. She wanted her brother to leave with her at once. When he insisted on first obtaining authorization from Brother L'Heureux, she became indignant and demanded an explanation. For Marie de La Salle and her uncle, and for the members of the clergy who would be present at the reception, it was unthinkable, even intolerable, that Father de La Salle, Doctor in Theology and former Canon of the Cathedral of Reims, should have to obey a Brother, an ordinary layman of no background or social standing.

Alerted about this strange situation, the Archbishop of Reims, Monseigneur Le Tellier, upheld the point of view of Father de La Salle's critics and immediately proceeded to invalidate the election, obliging our superior to remain at the head of the community.

Seeing that there was no way, for the time being, to prevent this interference on the part of the Archbishop, Father de La Salle submitted to the decision. He decided, however, that he could overcome the opposition by having one of the Brothers ordained a priest who could then become the superior. Father de La Salle himself would later step down from the position of superior and yet would not be under a layman. This clever scheme would circumvent the objections of the Archbishop. Father de La Salle immediately chose Brother Henry L'Heureux and asked him to begin his studies for the priesthood.

This decision surprised me. Though not at all jealous of Brother Henry and not wishing to become a priest myself, I could not help but think that this would not solve the problem. Wouldn't the Archbishop feel thwarted and challenged? Once Brother Henry was ordained, wouldn't his Excellency consider him, too, subject to his authority? Would he not then feel authorized to interfere in our community, with even more vigor, perhaps, since he had been outsmarted by Father de La Salle? Our superior, evidently, did not consider the matter in this light. He was blinded, perhaps, by his extreme desire to give up his position of authority and to live a more quiet life, doing priestly work for the poor, while living with us and helping us with advice and encouragement.

Things were not quite the same in Reims after these events. Since Father de La Salle did not want the new Society to be controlled by the Archbishop of Reims, he considered once more an offer he had received from a pastor in Paris over a year ago to open a school in the capital city. He had gone to Paris many months before to visit his brother, Jean-Louis, who was in the seminary there, and had been asked by the parish priest of Saint Sulpice to send some Brothers to take over the parish school. It was the very same school on Princess Street that I had known so well as a boy. Father de La Salle had promised then to send two Brothers when he could.

The offer was providential, he thought, because it would take him away from Reims and leave Brother Henry L'Heureux in a position of authority during his absence. He considered this step as one of the utmost importance for the future of our Society. It would free him at last from all family ties and social obligations in Reims, from the ties that still linked him to his former colleagues, the Canons of the Cathedral, and especially from the ecclesiastical ties that bound the Society to a single archdiocese. The Archbishop of Reims tried by every means to prevent the departure of Father de La Salle. He went so far as to promise our superior to finance the Brothers' schools in all the cities of his archdiocese, if we would stay in Reims. Even this magnificent offer did not tempt Father de La Salle, whose vision saw the Brothers working beyond Reims and whose trust in Providence was without limits.

Archbishop Le Tellier finally gave Father de La Salle permission to go to Paris.

8

On a cold winter's morning of February 1688 three of us started on the road south toward Paris. Before leaving Reims, Father de La Salle, Brother Antoine, and I, had lingered at the cemetery where our Brothers were buried. Our remembrance of Brother Bourlette and the other Brothers resting there was to be a source of courage and determination during the days of travel. A journey from Reims to the capital, on foot, in the middle of winter was no light undertaking. I appreciated the company of Brother Antoine all the more, since Father de La Salle always walked a little ahead of us.

Then, too, Antoine had a way of finding something to eat when the time came. We would stop to rest and he would be off to locate the priest of the village or someone in the market place who could satisfy our needs. As frugal as our meals were on these occasions, I wondered how many thousands of hungry mouths in the city were having as much.

The closer we got to Paris, the more people we met on the road, all heading in the same direction. War and famine had reduced most of them to utter poverty. They were hoping no doubt to better their lot in the capital. One old man and his son, intrigued by our strange appearance, walked with us for a short while as we entered the city. When he learned we were going to Princess Street, he couldn't hide his astonishment.

"That section of the city is no place for the likes of you," he said. "It has a bad reputation."

"We'll try to give it a better one, if we can," Father de La Salle answered.

At that the old man turned aside shaking his head as much as to say: "You're out of your mind if you think you can do anything about it."

Once within the city limits of Paris, we easily reached the parish rectory at Saint Sulpice and were told that the pastor, Father de La Barmondière, was at the school. On arriving there, we found the street door wide open and no one in the passageway leading to the classes.

Then, of a sudden, the silence was broken by loud screaming coming from a classroom to the right, ahead of us. The sound was familiar to me. If Rafrond were still here, he must be up to his old tricks again, I thought.

As we hurried to the door, it opened of itself and Rafrond stepped out, almost bumping into Father de La Salle. I recognized him at once. It was the same old Rafrond who ran the school years ago.

"Excuse me, your Reverence. You see, I thought for a moment you were Father de La Barmondière. I've had to punish one of the lads and I was going to fetch the Pastor. You couldn't by any chance be Father de La Salle? I remember when you came to teach catechism here years ago. I am Rafrond, you will remember. I'm in charge of the weaving shop now. Father Compagnon is the director of the school. You came just in time. Thanks to you, I can breathe freely again, at least for a while."

"Monsieur Rafrond, this is Brother Antoine and Brother François. Maybe you remember Jacques Delanot. He came to school here as a boy."

"That little rogue! I can't believe it. Are you going to take over the classes? I knew some new teachers were coming, but I had no idea they would look like you. Excuse me if I say your attire is a bit strange. It won't help you any. You don't know what you're getting into, Monsieur de La Salle. These youngsters are a bunch of scamps and nothing more. They're worse than in the days of Delanot. The only language they understand is the rod. When you want to get results with them, just remember that."

"There must be some other way."

"I speak from experience, mind you. Take my word for it."

De La Salle and two Brothers take over a charity school in Paris to the great dissatisfaction of Monsieur Rafrond.

"We shall see. Now, could you tell me where I can find Father de La Barmondière?"

"Of course. Come this way."

Father de La Salle followed Rafrond down a corridor and finally into a room at the back of the building. Brother Antoine and I waited in an empty classroom.

"What a reception!" Antoine said. "It looks like we're going to have trouble. It's one thing to open a new school and run it the way Father de La Salle does, and quite another to step into someone else's boots."

"You're right. At any rate, it's going to be an interesting experience. I'm willing to give it a try."

Father de La Barmondière was delighted that we had arrived at last. He introduced us to the curate, Father Compagnon, who graciously showed us around the school. By evening that first day, we had visited almost every room and corner of the building that was to be our new home. Monsieur Rafrond and his assistant, Maurice, had shown us the weaving shop and had explained how important it was for the school.

The shop opened into a narrow courtyard paved with cobblestones. From this yard, a spiral stairway led up to the different levels and to a labyrinth of rooms and passageways to left and right. At the very top, under the roof, were several small rooms where we were to be lodged. Monsieur Rafrond and Maurice had rooms in the same building, on the floor below, along with a ten-year-old orphan boy by the name of Paul Narra. Father de La Salle chose the smallest and most inconvenient room of all, wedged in a corner close to the stairway. Antoine and I were given rooms toward the middle of the hallway.

We had never lived in such close quarters before, not even at Father Dorigny's parish house in Reims with Monsieur Nyel. Besides being crowded within, we were exposed to the neighbors on all sides. It was a very short time before we became aware that they took a kind of malicious pleasure in watching our every move. We couldn't step out into the courtyard or into the street without having their curious eyes fixed on us.

And so, under these strained conditions, we started a new kind of life in Paris. The first week saw little better than pandemonium à la mode. We were not at all used to other people interfering with our work, because Father de La Salle had always had a free hand to organize and direct things for us. Here the situation was very different. Father Compagnon was the director of the school and he didn't seem in the least inclined to allow his authority to be questioned.

Monsieur Rafrond ruled his little domain at the expense of the youngsters who worked for him, although they were supposed to be learning the weaver's trade. Maurice was called Rafrond's assistant but Rafrond used him as a kind of messenger to execute his own orders. I could see that Maurice obeyed Rafrond reluctantly and would much rather have taken orders from Father de La Salle, who quickly won him over to our way of seeing things. Maurice agreed to help with the classes when he was not occupied in the shop and, all in all, took great interest in our work.

The school suffered terribly from the irregularity and disorder that Father Compagnon and Monsieur Rafrond tolerated. The students didn't have to come on time and could leave when they wanted. New students kept arriving and our classes were often interrupted. Sometimes Father Compagnon changed the schedule or simply dismissed the classes. Father de La Salle was frustrated and disturbed.

After a month in this predicament, I was beginning to feel that I couldn't go on much longer. The days in the classroom brought me no consolation and I couldn't rest at night. Although Antoine in all his good-heartedness tried to keep me from getting discouraged, my enthusiasm weakened from day to day. Sometimes I even asked myself if I had not made a serious mistake in accepting Monsieur Nyel's offer and getting involved with him in the first place. Why didn't Father de La Salle do something about it?

Things really came to a head one afternoon when our superior happened to be away on business in the city. Brother Antoine and I were to take the catechism classes while Monsieur Rafrond took a third group to the weaving shop. I had hardly begun my lesson when a chorus of unusual voices coming from the street caught my attention. Looking up, I saw Father Compagnon disappearing past the window, waving both arms in front of him as if he were herding a bunch of goats. The door burst open a few seconds later and in came five or six lads, all bent down, bumping into each other and uttering strange monosyllables. The priest pushed the last of them into the classroom as if glad to be rid of them, pulled the door closed again and continued on his way down the street.

The newcomers brought the number of my pupils up to forty. The number hadn't been the same for a single day since I had taken over the class. One day I had seventy students crammed into the room. Today I simply tried again to get on with my lesson, but just then the church bells of Saint Sulpice began to ring, loud and strong. As if this had been the signal agreed upon, eight or ten boys jumped up excitedly and dashed for the door.

"Wait a minute," I shouted. "Where are you going?"

"We're the altar boys," yelled one of them. "We'll be late. We'd better run. It's a funeral!"

In the confusion, several benches toppled over and it took five to ten minutes for things to settle down again. I think all the class would have gone out into the street if I hadn't taken up a position at the door as quickly as I could to put a stop to the exodus.

Then what do I see but old Rafrond in the courtyard sticking his head in the window. From what I could gather, one of the looms in the shop had collapsed and he needed a dozen or more of the bigger boys to help him set it up straight again. Before I could cross the room, they were up and gone—some through the side door, some out the window.

As far as I was concerned, that was it! There was no use fighting any longer.

"You can go home, all of you," I shouted in anger and disgust, "and don't come back until tomorrow. That is, if you find the door open."

No one moved. A strange silence came over the pupils who were left in the room. They clung to their benches as if for dear life.

"What are you waiting for? I mean it!" I banged the table, "Get out!"

A few got to their feet slowly and moved toward the door. Then, one by one, the others followed. All except little Paul Narra who sat there trembling and staring up at me.

"You too." I yelled. "Get out!"

He scampered away, half running, half stumbling, into the hall and up the stairs, not daring to look back.

I was alone at last, standing with my back to the closed door, trembling and fearing that Father de La Salle might come back any minute. What could I tell him? How could I make him understand?

I stood there for a long while, waiting for the lesson time to expire, listening to the monotonous sounds from the weaving shop, and watching evening shadows invade the courtyard. Then I slipped out into the street and walked away slowly with a mind to reach the public square. But I soon discovered there was no way I could escape, either from the curious eyes of people idling in the street or from the innermost thoughts that racked my brain.

With every step that took me further away from the school, my panic increased. I couldn't help but hear the jeering remarks that bystanders made about me because of the way I was dressed. One ugly looking individual came straight up to me and blocked my way. He had a wine bottle in his hand.

"What kind of priest are you, anyway?" he mocked. "Do you want a swig? You'd better take that robe of yours off before the bishop catches you." He laughed hilariously as two other hecklers joined him. In fact, a crowd was beginning to form in the middle of the street.

I was at my wit's end and probably would have been dragged into a tavern and drenched with cheap wine had I not discovered a way to escape. Near the corner of the street a hand-cart was parked in front of a cloth shop, leaving just enough room for one person to get by. I squeezed into that space and managed to reach the shop entrance. Someone grabbed my arm and pulled me into the shop just in time to close the door in the face of my pursuers.

I stumbled and fell into a pile of wool in the middle of the room. Looking down at me with a big smile on his face was Maurice from the weaving shop.

"You're welcome, Brother François, but I hope you won't stay lying on that pile of wool all evening. Monsieur Rafrond is waiting for it in the shop. What on earth brought you here, anyway?"

"You did, if I am not mistaken," I said, trying to laugh. "I got very upset with everything in school today and decided it was about time to get some fresh air."

"You were lucky this time, but be careful. That group out there has been causing trouble in the neighborhood for weeks. One of these days the police will have to step in. If you do go out, don't wear that outfit of yours. It attracts too much attention. I'll give you something different to wear, if you like."

"No, not now anyway. I'll be all right. Thanks, Maurice."

The noise outside had dwindled and the crowd was dispersing as the two of us watched from the shop window.

"You see that big fellow there? The one who came up to you in the street? His name is Potier, Marcel Potier. He's always hanging around this neighborhood, trying to see what's going on in your school. The Writing Masters sent him."

"Why?"

"The Writing Masters don't like what you are doing here. Don't you know? They have a monopoly on teaching writing. That's the way they earn their living. They don't want anybody else interfering. As soon as Father de La Salle and you Brothers came to the parish, they got very worried. You can be sure they'll keep an eye on you."

"The boys in our schools don't pay to learn how to write. Father de La Salle would never allow it."

"That's just it, you're depriving the Writing Masters of part of their livelihood and they're getting angry."

"But our pupils are too poor to pay. They could never go to the Writing Masters' schools."

"I know that. I'm just saying there's going to be trouble. Be careful."

Maurice took me into the back of the shop and showed me a kind of secret passageway by which I could get to the weaving shop and the courtyard without going back into the street. I felt relieved but at the same time ashamed. Nevertheless, I had made a discovery that had opened my eyes to the dire reality of our situation. We were soon going to have a war on our hands with the Writing Masters, if we kept on teaching writing. And perhaps with Monsieur Rafrond as well. Whose side would he take if trouble started in the school? One thing seemed clear. He was almost certainly exploiting our pupils in his weaving shop and making a handsome profit for himself by selling on the sly much of the cloth they made. Did Father de La Salle know?

As for myself, after the sad experience I had had in the street, I wasn't at all sure I wanted to get involved in any struggle that might arise. I had had enough already. I made my way back to the courtyard through the passageway Maurice had shown me, and then to the area near the weaving shop. I could see Rafrond in his shop, busy stacking and counting bolts of cloth, taking note of its fine quality, caressing it tenderly with his bony fingers, a self-contented smile on his face all the while.

The sight disgusted me, without my really knowing why. Or was I not rather just angry and disgusted with myself? I was sure that was the case when I got back into my classroom. The silence frightened me. The door to the street was closed as I had left it. The room was empty, the benches in order, but I could still see those little faces looking up at me, some frightened, some laughing, some crying.

I locked the door to shut them out for good, went into the hall and up the stairs to the first floor where we had our common study room. It was the place where Brother Antoine and I met with Father de La Salle, outside school hours, to read, to prepare our classes or to practice writing. Our superior was not there. He didn't go out often, only on urgent business and he seldom told us why or where he was going.

After the study hour, Brother Antoine and I took our frugal supper together in silence, as usual. Nothing in Brother Antoine's conduct showed any sign that he was aware of the afternoon's events or of my state of mind and heart.

I was no sooner in my bedroom for the night than the weight of it all fell on me as if the roof were coming down. All the tiredness that had been piling up for weeks swept over me. I sank down on my bed and stretched full length. Never had I felt so alone, so worthless, so abandoned.

I lit a candle beside my bed, hoping to chase away the phantoms that haunted me, but the flickering light only increased my anxiety by revealing the heavy beams that crossed the low ceiling, giving me the impression of being a prisoner awaiting execution. The heat in the room became oppressive, almost unbearable, or was it only the fever that was tormenting my whole being?

I got up and took off my robe, almost unaware of what I was doing. I stretched it over two hooks on the wall and arranged the white collar in place. At the sight of it hanging there, half in the shadows and half in the candlelight, I saw myself in the street and heard all over again the jeers of that merciless crowd and the mocking laughter of Marcel Potier. I sank my head into the folds of the robe and tried desperately to smother the sound of that ugly, drunken voice.

My hands came up with bits of black wool, and I thought of Maurice and the pile of wool on the shop floor. He must be in his room by now. I felt that I needed to talk to him again, to get things clear, perhaps to make some very important decisions. His room was at an angle from mine, on the floor below. I went to the window and got it open without making too much noise. It had been a rule to keep the shutters closed at night because of our neighbors, but I pushed them open too, for the first time since I had been in the room, and felt the soothing night air invade the narrow space. I discovered that I had been perspiring. My shirt was damp.

I could see the light of a candle burning in Maurice's room. In the distance, rising out of the dark, I saw the towers of the cathedral of Notre Dame, clearly visible and outlined in silver by the moonlight. From that same direction, I heard the sound of music. It seemed to be near the public square, beyond Princess Street. There were several stringed instruments playing and someone was singing, a woman's voice, in some tavern. The sound exerted a sensual and mysterious attraction that I found hard to resist.

I sat on the edge of my bed just long enough to take off my heavy, clumsy shoes and put on my sandals, then crossed to the door. It squeaked and rattled as it came open, I slipped into the hall and waited in the darkness to get control of myself. I started toward the spiral staircase, but after a few steps I had to catch my breath. A sudden feeling of nervousness took hold of me and I began to tremble.

I knew that at the next turn in the hall, a few yards from the stairway, I would have to pass directly in front of Father de La Salle's room. Had he returned? The thought disturbed me.

The door to his room was open, but I saw no one. A candle on the table was burning brightly. I looked up and discovered myself reflected in the window at the end of the room. My shirt and pants were like those worn by Vuyart that night in Reims. How could I ever forget! On the far side of the room, under the rafters near the bed, Father de La Salle was kneeling, his back to me. A large crucifix hung on the wall at the head of the bed.

As I lingered there in the doorway, hesitating, he lifted his head and looked toward the window. Our eyes met in the reflection for a brief moment—just long enough for him to fathom the very depths of my soul and for me to realize the truth about myself.

I lowered my eyes, ashamed. Stepping away from the door, trembling, I made my way back to my room and closed the shutters and the window. I knelt beside my bed and tried to remember the presence of God as he had so often told us to do. Peace finally overcame my troubled heart.

I had been with this saintly priest on several dramatic occasions in my life. This time, more than ever before, the experience was of momentous significance to me.

MORNING DAWNED BRIGHT. It was a spring morning at the beginning of May in the year 1688. Father de La Salle had wanted to say a special Mass in honor of the Virgin Mary because that day, he had said, was to be an important one for us. He said nothing about seeing me the preceding evening. I had regained my peace of mind and heart and was ready for whatever might happen. Brother Antoine and I went with Father de La Salle very early to the parish church. There, in the chapel dedicated to Mary, we prayed fervently and received holy Communion from his hands. At the end of Mass, we sang the Magnificat together, that beautiful hymn in honor of our Lady, composed of the very words Mary pronounced when she went to visit her cousin Elizabeth:

> My soul magnifies the Lord,
> And my spirit rejoices in God my Savior.
> He has shown might with his arm;
> He has scattered the proud in the conceit of their hearts.
> He has put down the mighty from their thrones
> and has exalted the lowly.
> He has filled the hungry with good things,
> And the rich he has sent away empty.

I was surprised at breakfast that morning, to see Father de La Salle so eager to be about the day's work, knowing as I did that he had probably passed most of the night in prayer.

"Brothers," he said, "I know how hard it has been for you these past few weeks. Forgive me for not having been able until now to do much about it. Yesterday evening, I had a long talk with Father de La Barmondière. It was not easy, but he has finally agreed to allow me to take whatever measures are necessary to establish order and discipline in the school. It will not be easy either to make Father Compagnon and Monsieur Rafrond understand this, but I trust, with God's help, that things will improve little by little. Otherwise, we shall return to Reims." Then he added quite simply but firmly "We have no other choice."

He could see that we were pleased.

"To begin with, we are going to decide on one very important rule, perhaps the most important of all. The door to the street is to be closed and locked at eight o'clock. The children who are present will follow your lessons as usual. No one is to be allowed to leave class and no one is allowed to enter class during school hours. The boys will soon learn, and their parents as well, that they must be on time."

"But what if Father Compagnon comes as he always does?" Brother Antoine objected.

"I shall be here to meet him and see that this regulation is strictly observed."

" And what about Monsieur Rafrond?" I said. "He interrupts the classes three or four times a day."

"I have already tried to make it clear to him that your classes come first. We shall take care of the weaving problem in due time. I am not at all against the boys' learning to weave. Some day, and I hope soon, we will be able to teach them not only weaving but many other trades as well. For the time being, no one is to go to the shop."

He stood up. "Let us go now, each of you to your own classroom. The boys who arrive first may practice writing at their places, in silence, or they may play in the courtyard. No one in the street. I'll go myself to welcome the youngsters. Brother François, from your classroom, you may want to keep an eye on those in the yard. At eight o'clock, when I ring the bell, all the boys will go to the yard. They will form two groups and you will check the attendance. Then you may start your lessons just as you used to do in Reims. God be with you."

He left us and took up his place near the corner of the building where a small group of boys had already gathered. We watched from a distance, admiring the way he had with them.

"Look at that," Brother Antoine remarked. "How he loves to be with those youngsters, and how well they like him! He is really himself this morning. I knew he wouldn't let things go on as they were. Good luck, François."

Several boys were already seated in their places when I entered the room. They looked up at me with inquiring eyes. One of them said:

"The door was open, Brother François, so we came in. Was that all right?"

"Of course it was all right, but we won't start the lesson till eight o'clock. Now, is that all right?"

Another voice sounded from a bench near the window. "Are you still mad at us, Brother François?" It was little Paul Narra.

"No. That was yesterday. Today is another day. If some of you want to play in the yard, you may do that until eight o'clock when the bell rings."

At that moment, I saw Maurice coming through the yard toward me. I went to the window to meet him.

"Good morning, Brother François. I see you have recovered from yesterday's adventure."

"Yes. Thanks again. I don't know how I would have managed without your help."

"What is this I hear about no more help in the weaving shop? Monsieur Rafrond is very disgruntled."

"It's only for a short time, I think, so that Father de La Salle can get the school organized and running properly. He's not at all against weaving classes. You can be sure of that."

"I just wanted to tell you that I'll be very busy in the shop if the boys don't come anymore. I won't be able to help you much. But I promise to keep an eye on Marcel Potier. Remember what I said."

From the window, I watched Maurice go back to the shop, where Monsieur Rafrond was waiting for him impatiently. Several of my pupils were standing nearby, listening to their conversation and waiting to see exactly what Rafrond would do. After some arguing with Maurice, Rafrond pushed him into the shop angrily and beckoned the boys to follow him. Three of them went inside.

Just then, Father de La Salle appeared at the door, bringing in with him the last stragglers from the street. He sent them to the courtyard, locked the door to the street and made a sign for me to meet him outside. When the last of my pupils were in the yard, I joined Father de La Salle. It seemed as if there were many more youngsters than usual this morning. I thought at once that word might have gotten around about my sending them home the day before and now they had come out in full force, mostly through curiosity, no doubt.

Father de La Salle rang the school bell and the noisy crowd came quickly to order. It was impressive to see him standing there amidst all those youngsters. There was no question about it. He loved them and they loved him.

He came over to me and said quietly:

"I don't see René Lafarge or Pierre Quentin or Jacques Rivois. I said hello to them this morning in the street as they came in. Do you know where they are?"

"I saw them go into the weaving shop with Monsieur Rafrond a short while ago, Father. Do you want me to go and get them?"

"No, Brother, I'll go myself."

He crossed the yard and entered the shop without the least hesitation. Everyone was watching him. No one moved. In a few moments he came out with the three boys. René Lafarge was in the lead. Father de La Salle followed, his right arm around the shoulders of Pierre Quentin and his left around Jacques Rivois. Behind him, Monsieur Rafrond stood in the doorway of his shop, his hands on his hips and face red with consternation. The boys came over to me and joined the group.

Without saying a word, Father de La Salle got the two class-es to line up two by two, making signs to show them what he wanted, one group in front of me and the other in front of Brother Antoine. And so we entered our classrooms.

Throughout the day, Father de La Salle seemed to be every-where and yet he did not once interrupt or disturb our classes. He went to the street where several boys were waiting to get in. He must have succeeded in explaining the new regulation to them, because they went away quietly. Then I saw him return to the weaving shop to talk to Monsieur Rafrond and Maurice.

Finally, toward the end of the morning, Father Compagnon appeared, accompanied by two boys and their parents. He found the door locked but Father de La Salle was there quickly to open it and meet the little group. He had them wait in the small room that served as a parlor, while he went to ring the bell announcing the end of the classes for the morning.

The boys from Brother Antoine's class came out first, in double file and waited in the street for him to dismiss them. Then mine followed. Our superior watched all the while, saying a kind word to the boys who came up to him. When all was calm again and the boys had all dispersed, he came back to the parlor, asking me to remain with him. Father Compagnon started the conversation:

"Monsieur La Salle, these parents are complaining that the Brothers refused to accept their children in school this morning. Don't they have as much right as anyone else to come here?"

"Of course they have a right, Father. No one is denying that. Brother François here will be glad to have them in his class, but he has some rights too. The boys must be here on time. From now on, the doors of this school will close at eight o'clock. Nobody will be admitted any later. I shall see to that myself. It was I and not the Brothers who refused them this morning."

"And what about my son?" one of the ladies said, pointing to her boy standing near me. "He was supposed to work in the weaving shop this morning. I pay Monsieur Rafrond every month so that he can learn to weave."

"I am surprised to hear that, Madame. There must be some misunderstanding. From now on, no one will have to pay to come to this school, not even to learn weaving."

"Monsieur de La Salle," interrupted Father Compagnon, "what are you saying? Do you not realize that the parish makes a considerable profit from the weaving shop? We use that money to help the poor."

"There are other ways to help the poor. I'm sorry, Father, but the boys will not go back to work in the shop until the school is properly organized and until the Brothers and I have had the time to study their aptitudes and to decide who are really interested in learning the trade. Then I shall see to it that they are properly trained and that they pay nothing for their training."

"That is foolish," Father Compagnon said in a mocking tone. "I shall take the matter up myself, with the proper authorities, before the week is over. You shall see. Good day, Monsieur de La Salle!"

He turned to leave and the others followed. One little fellow lingered for a moment. Then, tugging at Father de La Salle's sleeve, he looked up and said:

"Can I come to school this afternoon, Monsieur de La Salle?"

"Indeed you can, but don't be late. Remember, the door closes at two o'clock."

"It wasn't as difficult as I had expected," Father de La Salle said as he turned to me and smiled. "Let's join Brother Antoine for our noonday meal."

And that was the way the morning ended.

The following days were pleasant in the classes. The pupils came regularly and in greater numbers than ever before. Nevertheless, there were several shadows in the picture. One was Monsieur Rafrond. Not only was he unhappy about the changes, but he became openly hostile to us and to the school. For a time he tried to run the shop with the help of Maurice alone. Then he stopped coming altogether. Father Compagnon showed his anger by siding with Rafrond. They were often together and sometimes with Marcel Potier.

One night, about two weeks later, shortly before the summer vacation, Father de La Barmondière, the pastor of Saint Sulpice, sent a messenger, a priest named Father Baudrand, to tell Father de La Salle that he and the Brothers were no longer needed in Paris. Father de La Salle was ordered to turn the school over to Father Compagnon. We were dumbfounded. Brother Antoine and I pleaded with Father de La Salle to let us go to the pastor ourselves. If he didn't listen, we would go to the Cardinal. We would organize all our pupils and their parents. They could surely make him listen to us. The school was doing well; we were absolutely sure of that. There had to be some mistake.

Father de La Salle, however, would hear nothing of it. He considered every word of the pastor as a command and, though Father de La Barmondière had given no reason for the sudden order, Father de La Salle asked us to be ready to leave the next day. As a last resort, we agreed to pray together for a longer time that night. Perhaps the pastor would change his mind.

The following morning we went to Father de La Salle's Mass, thinking that it might well be our last in Paris. After the closing prayer, Father Baudrand came into the sacristy and asked our superior to accompany him to the rectory to say good bye to the pastor. Brother Antoine and I returned to the school alone, disillusioned and disheartened. The morning seemed to drag on into eternity as we watched and waited for Father de La Salle to return. And then we saw him coming down the street with a little crowd of children around him. We opened the door for him when he had said good-bye to his young admirers.

"God be blessed!" he said. "The pastor has changed his mind. You see how very good your prayers were. You have won a real victory. Thank you both."

Without saying more, he hugged each of us like a father and then turned quickly away to go to his room. I could see that he was overcome by emotion, and I understood that he wanted to be alone.

Brother Antoine and I were delighted.

"Come along," I said to him. "Let's find Maurice. Remember, we have to learn how to make those looms work. We've got to reopen that shop this summer."

Several weeks passed before we learned what had provoked the crisis. For one thing, the innovations that Father de La Salle had introduced to the school brought such good results that he came to be considered a dangerous competitor by other teachers in the parish, especially the Writing Masters who were losing fee paying students. The boys in our school were now grouped into several classes according to age and ability. They followed the same lesson all together instead of being taught one by one, as was the custom in other schools. This not only saved time but prevented disorder. Definite periods were assigned for the teaching of religion, writing, reading, and arithmetic. Much emphasis was given to Christian behavior. Father de La Salle had written a book for this purpose, He called it *The Rules of Christian Decorum and Civility* and we were using the first chapters to practice reading in French. This was Father de La Salle's most revolutionary innovation—the teaching of reading in French instead of Latin. Father Compagnon was annoyed because of this innovation and because he could no longer interrupt the classes or have the youngsters at his beck and call. But the real reason for the crisis went deeper than this.

Jealous and evil tongues had accused Father de La Salle of serious misconduct in the direction of his community and the parish school. These reports had been spread throughout the parish and came to the ears of the pastor, Father de La Barmondière, who at first believed them. Fortunately for all of us, he learned the truth behind all these attacks and changed his mind before it was too late.

Once this storm had passed, our school became more and more popular in the neighborhood. It was so crowded that Father de La Salle decided to bring three more Brothers from Reims. He chose Henry L'Heureux, Nicolas Vuyart, and Gabriel Drolin. We were thus able to start another class and to reopen the weaving shop, which prospered more than ever before. Brother Henry helped in school when he could but also continued his studies for the priesthood.

That next year, Father Baudrand became the new pastor of St. Sulpice. He held Father de La Salle in great esteem and very quickly asked him to open another school in the parish. This further aroused the jealousy and anger of the Writing Masters, who determined to chase us from Paris once and for all.

One morning, four or five men forced their way into my crowded classroom just after classes had begun. They were accompanied by the chief of police. I recognized Marcel Potier among them and realized quickly what I was up against. He began pushing the boys roughly from their places and snatching the writing materials away from them. They were frightened and gathered around me for protection. I felt utterly helpless. At that moment, Father de La Salle entered the room and came face to face with Potier.

"Sir, what is going on here? There is no need to put your hands on those children. They are under my protection."

Potier stopped short. "Why ask me? Ask the representative of the law. I'm only following orders."

The chief of police spoke up to defend Potier and the others. "An official complaint against you has been filed with Monsieur Claude Joly, the executive in charge of the schools in Paris. The law forbids you to teach writing. I have been sent by the magistrate to collect all the writing materials in the school."

"The law may protect the Writing Masters," Father de La Salle answered forcefully. "They may collect fees for teaching writing, but there is no law that forbids the teaching of writing in charity schools. How would the poor ever learn to write if the law forbade it? No injustice is being done to anyone here. The boys here pay no fees."

"The poor! What right have they to an education?" the officer answered angrily. "Let them work for a living."

"The poor have the same rights as the rich. It's unfortunate that they don't have the same possibilities, but it's not their fault. I ask you to return those materials. They belong to the school. Monsieur Claude Joly has no authority whatsoever here. This is a charity school. It depends on the pastor alone. The law is very clear about that."

"I have orders to confiscate these materials and I intend to do so, Monsieur de La Salle. You have a right to appeal to Parliament if you wish, in which case, if you win, the materials will be returned to the school. Until such time, let me warn you, any further violations of the law may prove very costly."

The group left the school, carrying away most of the writing materials. Father de La Salle was not intimidated. He spent several weeks preparing a defense and appealed to Parliament. He astonished the court with the clarity and logic of his presentation and won the case. The writing materials were returned but the jealousy and hatred of our rivals only increased. This was the first of a long series of conflicts we were to have with the Writing Masters.

10

WINTER THAT YEAR brought with it all the inconvenience and suffering that poverty only helps to increase. Now that we had two schools in Paris, some of us had to go back and forth in the streets twice a day in every kind of weather. Father de La Salle often accompanied us. In truth, he did much more, because he was frequently called to visit the sick and dying in the neighborhood near our schools. This had been his labor of love in Reims and now he gave himself to it again with great zeal. Such exposure to the cold and dampness of the Paris streets brought on severe attacks of rheumatism, which left him weaker each time he went out. We had not forgotten the incident in the snowstorm that had almost cost him his life in Reims, and we were frankly worried about his condition.

The crisis came even sooner than we had expected. Father de La Salle had been called to the Bastille one afternoon to minister to a poor priest who was imprisoned there. He had found the condemned man clothed in rags, half frozen and very near the point of death. He wrapped him in his own cloak, prayed with him for a long while and then returned to Princess Street through a bitter storm. Because of his rheumatism, he could hardly walk by the time he reached the house. In spite of his fatigue and pain, he had supper with us and then joined us for community prayer, asking us to pray for the dying priest he had visited and whom he had helped make his peace with God.

Although Father de La Salle often retired very late, it was a regulation in our community to rise at half-past four in the morning and to meet in our common room for prayer and meditation. On occasion, he would use this time to teach us how to make mental prayer or to tell us about the life of the saint we honored that day or to explain some aspect of our religious life. That particular morning, I had come down to the common room earlier than usual. I had made it a habit to be among the first there, ever since that unfortunate night when I had tried to leave the house unobserved. I had always found Father de La Salle kneeling there at his place near the statue of Our Lady in the front corner of the room. He usually kept a vigil lamp burning there. This morning the room was in almost total darkness. There was no lamp burning and, unless my eyes were deceiving me, there was no one kneeling there in our superior's place. I lit a candle near the crucifix on the front table.

No, Father de La Salle was not there. The other Brothers began to take their places here and there in the semi darkness. I watched them as they entered. Each one noticed the empty place and cast an inquiring glance in my direction. Had Father de La Salle gone? Had something happened during the night?

"Brother Gabriel," I whispered. "I'm going up to his room. Come with me. I have a strange feeling that something has gone wrong."

Taking a candle from its holder on the wall, I led the way up the winding stairs to the third floor. The stairs creaked. A sudden gust of cold wind entering from a broken window pane made me shiver as I reached the landing. The room was there to the right, the door closed.

I called softly. "Father de La Salle."

No answer.

"Father, it's Brother François. Is anything the matter? May I come in?"

Still no answer.

Another gust of wind almost extinguished my candle. I turned the knob and opened the door, ever so quietly. In the dim light, I could see the table where a candle had long since burned its life away, and in the window I could see myself coming into the room. A feeling of fear swept over me.

I pushed the door back completely and stepped into the room. My eyes went straight toward the bed under the rafters. There, on the floor, in the same place I had seen him kneeling that night, lay the still, black form of Father de La Salle.

I bent over him and shook him a little. His hands were icy cold.

"Father, what is it? What's the matter?"

There was no response.

"Brother, help me get him onto the bed. Now go quickly and tell Brother Antoine to call Father Baudrand. Then get some hot coals to warm up this room."

After a few minutes Father de La Salle opened his eyes, trying to discover where he was and who was at his side. He reached to take my hand.

"It's you, Brother François. Thank God. I don't quite know what happened. I knelt down to pray. Then . . . I must have fallen asleep. I vaguely remember falling to the floor, but I was too weak to rise. Then that rheumatism. I could not move my legs at all. Even now, I . . . ."

"It was the cold. You have been exposed to it all night. Besides, you have not been well these last few weeks. You need rest."

Brother Gabriel returned with the hot coals and the room began to lose its icy chill. Father Baudrand also arrived, but there was little any of us could do. One of the Brothers brought a bowl of hot tea, which Father de La Salle drank slowly. It seemed to revive him somewhat. Several hours passed before the doctor arrived, but he too left us with very little hope. His only suggestion was to consult the renowned Dutch physician Helvetius, who happened to be in Paris at the time. We were able to contact him and were surprised and pleased to learn that he had heard of Father de La Salle and would be willing to see if anything could be done.

After examining the sick priest for a long while, Helvetius told us that he knew of only one possible remedy. Recovery was almost certain, if the patient could endure the treatment. If not, it would be impossible to save him. Facing such a terrible alternative, there was really no choice. Father de La Salle agreed to submit to the treatment and asked at once to be allowed to receive the sacrament of the sick.

Father Baudrand, who had stayed beside his fellow priest since early morning, went immediately to bring the Blessed Sacrament. Brother Vuyart accompanied him to the church, while I remained with the doctor to prepare what was needed. My heart sank within me as I became aware of the terrible ordeal Father de La Salle was about to undergo. A sort of grill was to be used, under which a bed of hot coals could be kept smoldering.

The coals were to be smothered with medicinal herbs. The vapor thus produced would contain the needed remedy, provided the sick person could withstand the heat long enough to let the vapors penetrate the paralyzed areas of the legs and back. "We'll just have to make sure he does not suffocate during this treatment," Helvetius said nervously.

When the doctor had finished preparing the room, he went for the needed medicines. From the window in the hallway, I could see him hurrying down the street. He was an amiable little man, but his tall wide-brimmed hat and long-tailed coat did give him a rather strange appearance.

Father Baudrand appeared at that moment, coming in procession from the church. Several other priests and seminarians had joined him and were carrying lighted candles. I could also see a small crowd gathering in the street in front of the school. These good people, who had learned to love Father de La Salle, had seen the procession and knew that all was not well. Brother Vuyart remained with the group outside when the procession entered our building.

We all knelt to recite the customary prayers with Father Baudrand. He then anointed Father de La Salle and gave him Holy Communion. Everyone stayed in the room, praying in silence, until the doctor returned. I saw tears in the eyes of the young seminarians when they were asked to leave. Even Father Baudrand was finding it hard to control his emotions. At the doctor's bidding, Brother Antoine and I went to fetch the hot coals.

When we returned, the patient was already stretched out on a low grill and covered with a heavy blanket. The treatment began at once. I shuddered at the thought of what he was enduring with that concentrated heat only a matter of inches beneath his exposed legs and back. The physician sprinkled the medicinal herbs on the coals every few minutes, causing the whole room to fill with fumes.

The treatment went on for more than two hours, during which Father de La Salle did not utter the slightest word of complaint. His eyes were closed, his breathing heavy, his lips sometimes moving in prayer. Finally, when Helvetius was satisfied that the treatment had taken effect, we helped him move the priest back to his bed. He was to be kept wrapped in heavy blankets and the room heated sufficiently to provoke abundant perspiration.

The remedy proved effective, for little by little Father de La Salle regained his strength. After three weeks of convalescence, he was able to resume part of his ordinary occupations. The recovery of our superior at a time when his presence was absolutely indispensable proved once again that Providence was taking care of us. If Father de La Salle had died, our young Society would probably have died with him.

11

THE SITUATION OF the community in Reims, during the absence of Father de La Salle, became very precarious.

In 1688 when we left Reims, there had been about fifty of us involved in the work. Now that number had dwindled to fewer than twenty. There were three groups: a community of Brothers who taught in the charity schools of the city, a training college for teachers, and a junior novitiate for young aspirants. These last two institutions were the first of their kind in all of France, and Father de La Salle was particularly fond of them. He realized that his own disciples would never be numerous enough to answer the crying need for teachers in rural areas throughout the country, and he knew, as well, that if he did not prepare young subjects to enter the Society, the number of his own disciples would never increase.

Brother Vuyart had been given charge of the training college in Reims and had accomplished wonders. After Father de La Salle called him to Paris, the college failed completely. As for the young aspirants, they needed to be near the Founder. He alone could inspire them with the noble ideals and courageous generosity needed to become a Brother. Father de La Salle was determined to bring the remainder of the group to Paris. For this purpose he rented the building next to our school on Princess Street.

During the two and a half years that we had been in Paris, some of the Brothers in Reims, Rethel, Guise and Laon had become discouraged and had abandoned the Society. Some had died of poverty and exhaustion. These were all convincing signs that our Society was fragile indeed and on the verge of ruin, despite ten years of heroic sacrifice and continual struggle. Now that Father de La Salle himself had been at death's door, he realized that other measures must be taken to consolidate the Society.

First of all, he began to prepare Brother Henry L'Heureux even more seriously to take his place as superior. Since his arrival in Paris, Brother Henry had finished his Latin and his theology and was nearly ready to be ordained a priest.

Secondly, our superior began looking for a house on the outskirts of the city where he could bring all the community together occasionally, and where he could open a novitiate to train new members of our group. This house would make our Society less dependent on the parish facilities of Saint Sulpice.

Then there was the question of our religious garb, which was forever causing trouble in Paris. Our pastor, Father Baudrand, admired Father de La Salle and appreciated our work in the schools, but he was quite unhappy about the way we dressed. He didn't like to see his parishioners laughing at us in the streets. He was continually nagging Father de La Salle to change our garb and have us dress like priests. Our superior would not give in. He even drew up a lengthy report on the origin and purpose of our Society in which he eloquently defended the religious garb he had designed for us. He wanted it to be clear that our vocation was decidedly different from that of the clergy. It was all important, in his mind, that the distinction in clothing be made.

It was about this time that Father de La Salle decided to return to Reims to visit the schools in that area and to encourage the Brothers there, one of whom was very seriously ill. We tried to convince him to put off his journey to a later date, because he had not yet completely recovered his own health, but his love for the Brothers in his native city was too great to keep him from returning to Reims. There the sick Brother died in his arms. Father de La Salle, exhausted and distressed, fell ill himself and had to delay his return to the capital.

In Paris, we felt alone and exposed to every peril. Then Brother L'Heureux suddenly took dangerously ill. The doctors were helpless. We contacted Father de La Salle by messenger, but he thought that we might be exaggerating the seriousness of the illness since Brother Henry had not been sick when our superior had left a few weeks before for Reims. Nevertheless, Father de La Salle started his return journey.

"Take me to Brother Henry," he said, on arriving in Paris and after greeting each of us. His features were so pale and he seemed so weak that we took him immediately to his room and obliged him to drink something hot and to rest. As soon as he lay down, he fell into a sound sleep until late the next morning. On awaking, he looked up at us in a startled manner.

"Why are you here with me? Where is Brother Henry?" he asked.

"I'm sorry, Father," I whispered, "but Brother Henry died three days ago. The doctors could not save him. There was no way." I tried to keep back my tears.

Father de La Salle sighed deeply, fell back onto his bed and, closing his eyes, wept silently.

Several days later, he told us that the sudden death of Brother Henry L'Heureux had been a sign from God. "There will never again be a priest in our Society," he said.

Paris in 1691 was no joyful place in which to live. We had found the capital teeming with poverty on our arrival from Reims in 1688, but now, with another war raging, there seemed no end of misery and misfortune. It was the English we were fighting again. No sooner had William of Orange come to power in England than war broke out in France. The poor bore the brunt of it. They swarmed into the slums of the Faubourg Saint-Marcel, loitered and disturbed the peace in the public square during the day, and shouted and caroused in the streets at night. In the face of such disorder, there could be no rest for the community of Brothers who inhabited the old school building on Princess Street.

Father de La Salle told us one day that he had found a quiet place in the country, called Vaugirard, that happened to be up for rent. He invited us to go there with him that very afternoon; he wanted to have our opinion before deciding to move from Princess Street. Thankful for the opportunity to get away from our crowded quarters in the city, to breathe the fresh country air, and to enjoy the beauties of nature, we set out with him—Brothers Drolin, Vuyart, Antoine, and I.

What a place this Vaugirard turned out to be! The house itself seemed in the last stages of dilapidation. It was not surprising that the owners were willing to let us rent it for very little.

The roof sagged, the doors swung loose on their hinges, the shutters were rotten and unpainted, and some of the windows were missing. Yet the large garden and the delightful shade about the place gave it an attractive appearance. The house contained very little furniture—only a few rickety old chairs, a lopsided table, one bed, and several benches. Everything was coated with dust and spider webs.

We were all disappointed, but, with the exception of Vuyart, we readily accepted Father de La Salle's suggestion that we use the summer months when not in school to work on the property and make the building habitable. The owners, we imagined, would be only too glad to get such an offer.

Brother Vuyart was disgruntled, claiming that we were already poor enough and would end up dying of starvation. I remembered how he had reacted in Reims at the time of the great famine and I wondered why he had returned to our ranks if he had not really had a change of heart. His opinion, however, did not prevail. Within weeks, friends of Father de La Salle had given him enough money to cover the lease and the cost of repairs and we came to take up permanent residence at Vaugirard.

Upon our entrance, a dozen or two scrawny little mice, the only occupants of the house, scampered away to hiding places in the wall. I wondered if they were not possibly rejoicing—if mice can rejoice—that new tenants had finally arrived, from whom they could pilfer their daily rations. I would like to have been able to tell them, then and there, that they would have to continue hungry if they expected to find anything extra in the Brothers' house. The real truth was that we were in almost as sorry a plight as they!

A number of young men from Paris came to Vaugirard to join us. I recalled that years back in Reims, some had joined the Society seeking their own comfort and were quickly disillusioned. Now, most of those who came were from relatively affluent families. They left their comfortable homes to share our poor one, where they had not even a bed to sleep in, where no warm meals were ever served, and where no fires were ever lit even in the coldest of winters. These young men found happiness and remained with us.

Thus, at a time when the Society seemed to be dying, Vaugirard began to give it new life. Father de La Salle sensed the importance of this moment. He chose two of his oldest and most experienced disciples, Brother Gabriel Drolin and Brother Nicholas Vuyart, and for two or three weeks prepared them in retreat to make a solemn pledge with him. The date chosen for the ceremony was the feast of the Presentation of Mary, November 21. Winter had set in early that year, 1691, the first winter we spent at Vaugirard. It had snowed during the night and scattered flakes were still fluttering in the early morning air as we made our way to the village church.

Father de La Salle, Brother Nicolas and Brother Gabriel knelt at the altar before the Blessed Sacrament, holding lighted candles in their hands. Their voices echoed down to us from the sanctuary.

> Most Holy Trinity, Father, Son, and Holy Spirit, prostrate with the most profound respect before your infinite and adorable majesty, we consecrate ourselves entirely to you and promise to devote ourselves unconditionally to the establishment of the Society of the Christian Schools, in the manner that seems most agreeable to you and most advantageous to the said Society.
>
> And for this purpose, I, Jean-Baptiste de La Salle, priest, and I, Nicolas Vuyart, and I, Gabriel Drolin, promise and vow to remain together until our dying day to procure and maintain the establishment of the said Society, even if only we three remained therein and were obliged to beg alms and to live on bread alone to see it through.

The ceremony made a very strong impression on all of us. I made the same vow with them, deep in my own heart, during the long silence that followed.

Brother Antoine told me afterwards that he too had the same thought. But there was something that bothered both of us. It was Father de La Salle's choice of Brother Vuyart to be one of the cornerstones, as it were, of our Society. Had our superior decided to put him to the ultimate test, overlooking the fact that he had deserted the community in Reims at one time and had been very critical of certain decisions made in common? We all knew that Brother Vuyart was an excellent teacher and a good administrator. He had proved that he was competent when he replaced Monsieur Nyel some years back. Perhaps Father de La Salle really had no choice but to count on him and on Brother Drolin, now that Brother Henry L'Heureux was dead.

We understood better just how much Father de La Salle trusted Brother Vuyart when, some time later, he put him in charge of a new foundation in Saint Hippolytus Parish. An opportunity had arisen there to open a teachers training college.

This type of work was very dear to Father de la Salle and no one seemed better fitted than Brother Vuyart to carry it out successfully.

Brother Gabriel Drolin was given an even more important mission. Father de La Salle sent him to open a school in Rome and thus hopefully establish a relationship that might eventually lead to the papal approbation of our Society.

We had reached the turning point in the history of our community and somehow we felt certain that nothing could ever destroy the fragile bark that Father de La Salle had launched on a very troubled sea. The vow that Brother Vuyart and Brother Drolin made with Father de la Salle was a summons to heroism for all of us, and this at a moment when our country was on the brink of another famine, more terrible and far reaching in its effects than the one we had already been through. This tragedy fell upon us in all its severity in 1692.

Conditions became very alarming at the schools. Each day I noticed new vacancies on the benches before me. I knew that these youngsters were paying the price of war in just as heroic a sense as were their fathers on the battlefields in the Netherlands. But what distressed me was my utter helplessness to do anything for them. I remembered that first famine in Reims when I helped Father de La Salle distribute bread to the hungry children that came to our classes. How different the situation now! How impossible to care for such a multitude! The parish of Saint Sulpice, the largest and most neglected in the city, resembled a huge anthill in which the poor and destitute swarmed by the thousands.

Acts of violence, which not even the police could control, increased in the city. Near one of our schools, the body of a small child was found by some passing merchants. The poor boy had been beaten severely. His flesh was torn and bruised. Word spread quickly throughout the neighborhood that he had been killed by his own parents who could no longer feed him. Incidents of this kind repeated themselves day after day. Paris became a city of living death.

The young men in the novitiate at Vaugirard experienced further privations. They depended entirely on friends in the city for their sustenance. Poor Brother Antoine, who made daily trips in quest of food, was so frequently robbed of his provisions before returning to Vaugirard that the famished occupants of the novitiate were actually on the verge of starvation. Finally, Father de La Salle brought them all to the school on Princess Street to live with us till the crisis was over.

One evening, Father Baudrand called on us with distressing news. He now found himself in the same sorry plight as all of us. His resources were completely exhausted, and he could no longer give us our usual stipend for our expenses. He suggested that we give up our community life for the time being and that we disperse, each of us getting along on his own, as well as he could. After Baudrand had left our house, Father de La Salle spoke to us very frankly.

"You have my permission to leave, if you wish, but let's not forget that there is still a good God in heaven. I am convinced that he will provide for us in spite of everything."

No one spoke. No one got up to leave. I noticed that Brother Nicolas Vuyart was not present that afternoon. Once again the thought of that night in Reims years ago when he had been the first to walk out came back to me.

We said prayers before meals over an empty table that evening, as we had been doing for two days. There was no miracle, no multiplication of the bread. In fact there was no bread to multiply. We went off to our rooms silently.

I couldn't sleep and I doubt that anyone in the house slept that night. I kept asking myself what Father de La Salle would do.

The next morning when he joined us for prayer, his countenance seemed even more serene than usual. Pleased to find everyone present, even Brother Vuyart, he assured us that all would be well because the King had sent a generous sum of money to Father Baudrand for the poor of his parish.

This good news was confirmed later that morning when our pastor returned to the school and promised to keep us supplied with food, as he had always done before.

By the summer of 1694, conditions had so greatly improved that Father de La Salle decided to call all the Brothers of the Society to Vaugirard to make a retreat together. The total number had dwindled. Some had died during the famine; others had deserted but, as a whole, our Society had now proved itself strong enough to resist the severest tempests. In testimony of this, Father de La Salle celebrated a special Mass of thanksgiving and allowed twelve of us to pronounce perpetual vows. We did this with the utmost solemnity, each in turn advancing to the altar where the Blessed Sacrament was exposed. Kneeling there beside Father de La Salle and holding a lighted candle in one hand, each of us

read the same formula of vows. When my turn came, I was deeply moved and must have walked to the altar very slowly as my
memory wandered back to that memorable night in St. Remigius
Church in Reims when I had pledged to follow Father de La Salle
the rest of my life. Now the time had come at last to do it offi-
cially. My voice trembled slightly as I began to read the text, but
the presence of Father de La Salle at my side inspired me to finish reading it with deep sentiments of faith and love.

Our superior had been the first to pronounce the words and
had remained at the altar until all of us had finished. The effect
that this act of consecration had on our community was tremendous. We were no longer just a group of men following Father de
La Salle and trying to teach as best we could. We were now a dis-
tinct Society composed of members who were committed for life
to carry out a special mission—the Christian education of
youth—and for this purpose to live together in community and
to obey the superior of the Society. The task ahead of us seemed
enormous but we were all the more happy and full of enthusiasm. After the ceremony, Father de La Salle called us to a special
assembly.

"Brothers," he said, "the ceremony of the vows this morning
was beautiful and consoling beyond words. I am proud of you
and congratulate you. You have taken a courageous step that will
greatly strengthen our Society; but now you must go still further
if you want to insure its future prosperity. You will come to realize, sooner or later, that it is not wise to have a priest as your superior. Besides, he who has occupied that position till now has
very poor health, as you know. Only a short time ago, he was
at death's door. God may choose to call him sooner than you
imagine."

He paused to see if we understood his words. Then he continued. "What I really mean to say is that you must have a Brother as superior. A priest will find it hard to understand your way of
life. Moreover, you will never be truly united if an outsider is allowed to be at your head; and this might well come about if the
matter is left unsettled much longer. I urge you, now, while we
are all here together, to elect a Brother, one among you as superi-
or."

We looked at one another in bewilderment. The same
thoughts must have been uppermost in all our minds. We remembered the confusion and discouragement that had occurred

in Reims and in Paris when Father de La Salle was not there. That would happen again if he were not the superior. Yet, no one dared raise any objection to his suggestion. We continued to listen.

"I'm asking you to think this matter over for a few minutes in silent prayer. Examine before God who among you is best fitted to be superior of the Society. Pray to the Holy Spirit and allow your choice to be influenced only by God's inspiration."

We prayed in silence and then cast our votes. Brother Nicolas Vuyart, being the oldest of the twelve, was delegated to read out the results. All the votes were for Father de La Salle, except one. The dissenting vote was for Brother Nicolas Vuyart himself. He read out his own name with such boldness that everyone in the room was shocked.

Father de La Salle spoke up at once, distressed that he had received so many votes.

"This is a very serious matter, Brothers," he said firmly and with a touch of impatience. "I think you ought to take into greater consideration the future welfare of this Society. I insist that you vote again, and I want you to choose one of your own number. I have been the superior too long. You need to take more control of the Society. Diocesan officials need to know that this new Society is going to last beyond my death and that it does not depend on them. Only an hour ago you vowed to remain in the Society for the rest of your lives. This is your Society and you should elect one of your Brothers to guide it."

I knew what Father de La Salle meant, but I was reluctant to see him step down. He had led us this far, often by the sheer force of his personality. He had managed to negotiate difficult situations with the clergy and with the Writing Masters. He was gentle and engaging with the Brothers, a real father. He had been firm when that was needed, but he had been kind in a Christ-like way. He had been a visionary through all these years, seeing possibilities where it had looked the bleakest and discovering ways to achieve his vision through the darkest tangle of conflict.

We proceeded to a new election, but if there had been any hope at all of electing one of the Brothers, it completely vanished with the first balloting. When the votes were read out, there was no dissenting voice. Father de La Salle was elected unanimously.

It was then that Brother Vuyart spoke out.

"Father de La Salle, allow me to say with all due respect, that you yourself made the vow of obedience with us, did you not? You must accept our decision."

Our superior finally broke the silence. "I accept," he said calmly, with great resignation in his voice. "But all of you must promise me this at least: in the future you must choose one of the Brothers. You must never choose anyone outside the congregation to be your superior."

The Brothers nodded in silence. Then, at his bidding, we drew up a memorandum saying that Father de La Salle was to be the last priest to serve as superior of the Society and that in the future only a Brother could be our superior. We all signed the document as Father de La Salle sat by, an expression of resignation tainted with sadness in his eyes.

12

DESPITE THE POVERTY and suffering that was ours at Vaugirard, our numbers continued to increase and our Society was becoming more unified than ever before. Father de La Salle wanted it firmly established, especially after the final commitment that twelve of us had made. He was adamant that we should organize our own life and work together with him, despite the continued opposition we had from Father Baudrand or perhaps rather because of it. We still needed letters patent from the King to give us legal status and to authorize us to own property and to run schools independently of the Writing Masters. We also needed the official approval of the Pope recognizing our association as a religious community and protecting us from any intervention on the part of local church authorities who might wish to change our rules and regulations. To help obtain this approval, Father de La Salle had sent Brother Gabriel Drolin to Rome to open a school there. He hoped thus to acquaint the Holy Father with the Brothers' work and convince him of its importance for the whole church.

To consolidate our work in Paris, our superior confided the supervision of our schools to Brother Jean Jacquot. This Brother had joined the Society in Reims when he was only fourteen years old and now at thirty he was an excellent teacher and director. When Brother Vuyart left Princess Street to become the director of the training college, Father de La Salle put me in charge of the school. Sometimes I would catch myself daydreaming as I watched the boys at work. I could still see old Monsieur Rafrond running around with a hickory branch, threatening us.

Maurice still helped us in the weaving shop, which was doing better than ever before. I was very happy and very grateful to be where I was and often thought of the part that Providence had played in my life. It was a great joy for me at this time to see one of my pupils become a Brother. When Paul Narra, the orphan lad we had found living at the school when we first came to Paris, turned eighteen, he asked to enter our Society. He had already been earning his own living for six years by his weaving and painting. With him came Theodore Sellier from Villiers-Le-Bel, the first of four brothers from the same family to enter our Society. His father was a very close friend of our superior. Paul and Theodore and another Brother by the name of Simeon Pajot were teaching with me at our School on Princess Street. More than one hundred fifty boys between the ages of ten and fourteen crowded our classes in such a manner that the old building seemed to be bursting at the seams. On weekends the four of us returned to Vaugirard to be with Father de La Salle.

On these occasions and during vacation times, I liked to help Brother Michael, who was the director of the novitiate. He had more than he could handle with better than twenty young men in formation there. I thus got to know him and them very well. He was a serious type of person, somewhat of an idealist, seeking ways and means to attain perfection rapidly. He often talked about Father de Rancé, the celebrated Abbot who had reformed the Trappist Order and whom Father de La Salle had consulted several times before making important decisions. Brother Michael seemed to want the novices to be like Trappist monks, which was not at all our vocation. He was really too severe with them, I thought. Father de La Salle could not get him to realize that being severe with oneself was one thing but trying to impose severity on others was quite another. As a consequence some of the novices got discouraged and returned to their homes.

My good friend Brother Antoine, who had come to Paris with me and was for a time in charge of the kitchen, was always afraid that the younger members of the community might leave because they never had enough to eat. He had developed great skill in teaching writing and drawing. His own penmanship was remarkable and many a Writing Master in Paris knew him because of it and envied him. Some of his former pupils now made their living by writing letters for people and by copying manuscripts.

Brother Thomas was also from Reims. He was four years younger than Antoine, very conscientious, devoted, and methodical. Father de La Salle had great confidence in him, entrusting him with many business matters concerning the community. It was he who often replaced our superior. We could not help but notice that Father de La Salle was more determined to share responsibility with us until he could succeed in having one of us elected in his place.

Supplying food for us all was now Brother Thomas's responsibility. And what a responsibility it was! Our numbers had increased so surprisingly that there was no longer enough room in the house to lodge another novice. But even more distressing was the fact that both age and the elements had reduced the building at Vaugirard to such a sorry state of dilapidation that it became unfit any longer for human habitation. We would have to find new living quarters. Father de La Salle confided this task to Brother Thomas, who went back and forth to Paris almost daily.

On one occasion as I was walking with him, we came upon an old deserted mansion on the outskirts of the city. It was a mansion not because of its splendor but because of its immensity, and it was deserted for the very convincing reason that it was haunted. At least so the neighbors said. The Luxembourg Gardens separated it from the city, adding to its isolation. An air of mystery hovered about the place. People said that strange noises could be heard within, that the enclosed garden held secrets beyond explanation, and that the ghosts of several old nuns buried there prowled about the lonely corridors at night. We had the good fortune several weeks later to meet the proprietors, who had still been unable to find any willing tenants. They seemed to welcome the opportunity of renting the place to Father de La Salle and the Brothers, provided of course that we could pay the lease on the property and keep up the rent. To our surprise, they were asking only 1600 pounds, but even this amount was beyond the possibility of a community as poor as ours. We would have to find some benefactor willing to furnish this sum.

In the meantime, something happened that obliged us to forget about the project of moving for the time being. Our pastor Father Baudrand fell seriously ill. The best doctors in Paris were called in but could do nothing for him. His illness finally ended in paralysis and he was obliged to resign as pastor of Saint

Sulpice. Though he and Father de La Salle had had many differences and misunderstandings, especially over our religious garb, they had great esteem and respect for each other. We had not forgotten how Father Baudrand had interceded for us when his predecessor, Father de La Barmondière, wanted to send us back to Reims and how as pastor he had been a real father to us when our superior was lying ill and very near to death. Brother Antoine and I went with Father de La Salle to visit him and to pray with him before he left Paris.

What did the future have in store for us now? Our schools in the capital were all located in the parish of St. Sulpice and depended almost exclusively on the support of the pastor. We waited, but not without a certain feeling of uneasiness, to see whom the Cardinal would name to succeed him. The choice fell on a priest by the name of Joachim de La Chétardye, who was the director of the seminary at Bourges, a city in the provinces quite far to the south of Paris. This priest had previously been professor at the seminary of Le Puy and was now sixty years of age. That made him fifteen years older than Father de La Salle. Though our superior told us that he had never met Father de La Chétardye personally, he had heard many fine things said about him from the Superior of the seminary, a holy priest by the name of Tronson, who was Father de La Salle's spiritual director. We learned that the new pastor had been affiliated to the Society of the Sulpician Fathers four or five years before Father de La Salle had come to the seminary of St. Sulpice in 1670 to study for the priesthood, but he had now been away from Paris for thirty years. During those years he had made a name for himself by his vast learning and his teaching, his simplicity of life, and his total devotedness to the seminarians under his care. This reputation preceded him to Paris. The King, who held him in great esteem, had offered him the bishopric of Poitiers, Father de La Salle told us. De la Chétardye's response had been: "Excellency, I have sixty good reasons for declining this honor and responsibility. At my age, I should not dream about anything except the sanctification of the numerous parishioners who will be under my care."

If we had felt somewhat uneasy after Father Baudrand's death, we were now reassured by what Father de La Salle told us. We would have a very saintly priest as pastor. The more I thought about the situation, the more I realized that Father de La Salle and Father de La Chétardye must be very much alike. They were both from noble families; they both gave up their wealth and their position in the world to become priests, devoting their lives to teaching. The one directed a seminary preparing young men for the priesthood, the other directed young men to become Brothers and teachers. Both were inspired by the same ideal of Christian living that was taught at the seminary of Saint Sulpice.

Would the two men get along well working together? Would Father de La Salle finally have someone on whom he could count unconditionally to back up our work? We awaited the arrival of the new pastor with impatience and when the day came we were delighted. Father de La Salle was among the first to go to the rectory to pay his respects. He took Brother Thomas with him. The rest of us were all busy in the classroom. Not only was Father de La Salle well received, but the new pastor took the occasion to congratulate our superior on having founded our Society and on the work the Brothers were doing in Paris. He said that he had heard much about this new Society of teachers and that he was eager to visit one of their schools. When told that the first school run by the Brothers in Paris was on Princess Street, only a few minutes' walk from the rectory, he insisted on going there immediately.

To my surprise, I saw the group approaching from the street and went at once to open the door. A small crowd began to gather. Some of the women with small children in their arms and other little ones trailing behind, pressed forward to greet Father de La Salle and to touch the hand of the new pastor. Brother Thomas had all he could do to keep the passage clear.

"How they must love you, Father de La Salle," the pastor said. "This is amazing."

"They have come to honor you, Father, not me. It is not every day a new pastor comes to the parish. Here is the school and here is Brother François to welcome you. Could you believe that he was here in school as a boy years ago when I was in the seminary? This is where we first met."

Father de La Chétardye looked surprised and pleased. Taking my hand he said kindly.

"Brother, I'm really very happy to meet you. I want to meet all the Brothers. Father de la Salle must be very proud of you."

"It is rather we who are proud of him." I said. "There is no one quite like him. Everyone loves him."

Father de La Salle interrupted me.

"Brother, please, show the pastor your class and then I will take him to the weaving shop."

The visit to my class took only a few minutes. Father de La Chétardye was evidently pleased. He thanked me sincerely before rejoining Father de La Salle to visit the rest of the school.

News of this first meeting with Father de La Chétardye spread very rapidly through our schools in Paris. At Vaugirard, Brother Michael and the novices waited with eagerness for the visit from the new pastor. It came some weeks later, after the pastor had had the opportunity of visiting the other schools and the training college. The result was the same. Everyone liked him.

As pleased as Father de La Chétardye was with the Brothers and the schools, it seemed that he could not get over the impression left on him by the state of utter poverty in which we were living at Vaugirard and on Princess Street. He made up his mind that he would do something about it, but in order not to seem to interfere directly or to criticize Father de La Salle, he chose to speak to Brother Thomas and to me one day when he was able to get us both to the rectory at the same time.

"Brothers, I am totally amazed, but edified of course, at how poorly you live. I have heard priests and bishops talk about your Founder and the sacrifices he made, but I never imagined for one minute that he had carried things this far. Have you always lived like this?"

"We have always been poor, Father," I said, "but not always as poor as we are now at Vaugirard. The house is too small for so many of us. We are happy though and it is rare to hear anyone complain. Father de La Salle has taught us to trust in Providence. On Princess Street, it is a different problem. We are only four there but we are constantly surrounded by the noise of the city and the indiscretion of our neighbors."

"I understand, Brother, but would your superior consider moving to another place? I feel sure he does not impose this poverty on you."

"Oh no," Brother Thomas said. "In fact, he is very worried about this situation. He is also worried about the health of the Brothers. He has asked me to look around for some other place and I have indeed found one which he likes very much, but it is entirely beyond our means, although the owner is asking only 1600 pounds rent."

"Where is it, Brother Thomas?"

"On the road to Vaugirard near the Luxembourg Gardens and the Carmelite convent. Several religious orders have occupied the building over the last twenty years, but for some reason or other none of them have stayed for any considerable length of time. There is a vast garden and courtyard, a chapel and a crypt where several nuns are buried. The house itself is very spacious. The property is surrounded by high vine-covered walls which

give the place an air of mystery. I must add, Father, but only jokingly of course, that I have heard strange stories about the place
and its former occupants, but I doubt that the Brothers would be
afraid of ghosts."

"Most interesting. This intrigues me a great deal, Brother
Thomas. Thanks to you, I shall have an interesting outing one of
these days. I assure you that I shall make it a point to visit the
property in the very near future and will keep you informed."

Brother Thomas and I were overjoyed at our meeting with
the pastor and the expectations it created.

"He seems to have taken a liking to you," I teased Brother
Thomas as we left the rectory. "Who knows but what you'll get
anything you want from him."

"I can hardly believe it, but, as you say, from our first meeting that day when Father de La Salle and I went to pay him our
respects, he has spoken to me several times, almost confidential-
ly, if that can be construed as a special liking. We do seem to get
along well together. But don't count too much on that. Besides,
you have your way of meeting people and getting things done
yourself. I'm only following your example."

"That's a compliment. We had best wait and see where all
this ends, don't you think?"

We did not have to wait long. Within two weeks, the pastor
called on Father de La Salle at Vaugirard one Sunday afternoon, a
time when it was customary for all the Brothers from Paris to be
there. He spoke with our superior alone for some time and then
asked to be allowed to speak to all of us.

"Brothers," he said, "I have what I think will be good news
for you. Brother Thomas has found a new residence which will
be much better suited to your needs than this poor old place. I
admire you for living under these conditions for so long. God
has evidently blessed you for it. Your Society is increasing in
numbers day by day and the five schools in our parish are flourishing beyond my fondest dreams. I have told Father de La Salle
that I will increase your annual stipend by 600 pounds and I
have found some generous friends in the parish who will make
monthly payments to help you cover the rent. They wish to remain anonymous. One lady whom you know very well, however,
and who greatly admires your work—I am speaking of Madame
Voisin—is offering 7000 pounds to buy furniture for the new residence. I asked Brother Thomas to see her and to explain the situation. You see how well he succeeded and how well he kept the
secret until today. I have spoken to his Eminence the Cardinal

about these changes and he is pleased with everything. He will allow you to enlarge the chapel that already exists in the house, covering the expense himself, and will authorize Father de La Salle to say Mass there daily for all of you. May God bless you in your new home and may he continue to bless your Society and your wonderful work."

We applauded spontaneously as the pastor finished his short speech. Father de La Salle, who was standing close by, embraced the pastor and thanked him in the name of everyone.

Thus, to the Grand'Maison—a name we gave the place because of its size—the novices came with the few belongings they had. The squeaky noises on the stairs made them wary at first and the hissing of the bats, high up in the rafters, caused not a little apprehension. But no ghosts appeared for some reason or other and, as much as we would have enjoyed a little excitement, we soon had to admit that the rumors we had heard were completely unfounded.

Our situation in Paris now seemed brighter than ever before. The Grand'Maison was spacious enough to house our entire Society. Father de La Salle decided at once to call all the Brothers there whenever possible to spend time with them and to help and encourage them in any way he could. Undoubtedly, he felt that with the favor shown by his Eminence, Louis Antoine de Noailles, the Cardinal Archbishop of Paris, and with the unquestionable backing of Father de La Chétardye, we could look to a bright future indeed as we settled down in our new home.

When the work on the chapel was finished, Father de La Salle invited a good friend of his, the Bishop of Chartres, Mgr. Godet des Marais, to celebrate a solemn Mass of thanksgiving and to bless the chapel and the other buildings. On this occasion our superior promised to send several Brothers to Chartres at the bishop's request to open charity schools in his city. Chartres was one of the favorite cities of Father de La Salle, perhaps because like Reims its beautiful cathedral was dedicated to Our Lady. People called it the blue cathedral because of its magnificent stained glass windows, the finest in all France.

Things went very well at the Grand'Maison for quite some time. The Cardinal paid Father de La Salle a singular mark of esteem by asking him to care for a group of Irish boys who had come to France in the company of King James II. Because of his strong attachment to the Catholic faith, the king had been exiled when William of Orange came to power in England. The boys were given a home in our house and Brother Jean Jaquot was placed in charge of their education. Father de La Salle taught them himself at times. The pastor and even the Cardinal came to visit them quite often and expressed their satisfaction.

Little by little, however, we noticed that Father de La Chétardye, who had been so very sympathetic toward us during the first months after his arrival in Paris, and to whom we owed so much, began to show signs of disagreement with Father de La Salle. They were little things at first, remarks about our clothing or about some school regulation or other. Why, for example, didn't we learn Latin so as to be able to teach our pupils how to serve Mass? One of the assistant pastors was in charge of the altar boys; it was not our job to train them.

I became involved in the discussions with Father de La Chétardye more than the other Brothers because I was so close at hand. He often came to the school on Princess Street and he never failed to give instructions of one kind or another which he expected to be carried out to the letter. He seemed to consider us his seminarians and, when Father de La Salle was not present, he acted as if he were our superior.

One day as the four of us were preparing to take our pupils to church to participate in a procession in honor of Our Lady, he appeared at our door. He was accompanied by one of the sacristans, who was carrying several white surplices draped over his arm.

"Brother François," he said, "I have brought these surplices for you Brothers to wear in the procession today. It is a very special occasion, you know."

I was caught by surprise. We all knew that our pastor did not like our religious garb, but it had never occurred to me that he might make an attempt to change it in this fashion. There was no time now to consult Father de La Salle. I would have to make the decision myself and probably suffer the consequences as well.

"Father," I said, "I'm sorry, but I cannot allow the Brothers to wear these surplices. Our superior would never approve of it. I thought that he had made that clear to you."

"I understand your attachment to Father de La Salle, whom you like to call your superior, but must I remind you Brothers that he is not the superior in the parish of Saint Sulpice? Neither is he a member of this diocese. You must remember this. Thus far he has been able to manage without being subject to local ecclesiastical authority in many important matters, but I intend to take the necessary measures to see that the right order of things is reestablished and that tradition is respected. Do you understand that, Brother François?"

"Yes, Father, but I still cannot allow the Brothers to wear the surplice, not even on this one occasion."

"Is that your last word?"

"Yes, Father, with all due respect."

"Then the Brothers are not to participate in the procession today. I shall send four seminarians over to replace you. They will lead the boys during the ceremonies. You Brothers may occupy one of the pews in the back of the Church if you wish. Thus the dignitaries who are attending the services will not take offense because of the way you are dressed. And, Brother François, I do not want you to think that I hold you responsible for this decision. I shall take up the matter personally with Father de La Salle at the first opportunity."

What a strange feeling I experienced in turning our four classes over to the seminarians who showed up some minutes later. They were, of course, impeccably dressed in long black soutanes and white lace surplices. The lads didn't know what to think but they remained silent and filed off two by two in perfect order. Several of them looked back at us standing in the street, as much as to say, "What's going on? Why aren't you coming with us?"

We watched them disappear at the corner and then made ready to set out ourselves. Our neighbors had noticed what had happened and some came up to greet us, asking if they might accompany us to church. Despite their company, we felt strangely alone. My thoughts were elsewhere when suddenly I found myself face to face with a man standing in the middle of the street as if to block my way. I had never quite forgotten that face, its ugly mustache, its cynical smile, the face of Marcel Potier. Today it reflected something else, a kind of vengeful satisfaction.

"So they have finally taken the lads away from you," he said jeeringly. "It's about time. La Chétardye knows what he's doing. At least he has the courage of his convictions. Pretty soon he'll be taking over the school, too, and you'll be in the street. Just mark my word, Delanot. But we could drink to that, couldn't we? Come along here, all four of you. There's no more room for you in church anyway."

Before I could answer, he had grabbed me and Brother Simeon by the arm and might have dragged us away with him if someone had not wedged his way between him and us, pushing

him all the way back to the door of the tavern. It was then I recognized Maurice.

"You talk too much, Potier," he said. "Go on back to your
wine and leave the Brothers alone."

"Thank you, once again, Maurice," I said. "You always seem
to appear at the right moment."

"Ever since your last meeting with this Potier—I hardly
think you've forgotten it—I've been keeping an eye on him. It's
time he begins to mind his own business."

"And you mind yours too, young fellow," Potier retorted.

"My business is with Father de La Salle and the Brothers and
the weaving shop, Potier."

I didn't catch Potier's last angry words. Everyone was shouting and pressing so close, he would have been crushed had he
not taken refuge in the tavern.

Maurice cleared the way for us and we hastened on to the
church where the ceremonies were beginning.

The day following this incident, things seemed to return to
normal. No seminarians showed up. We led the boys to church
in our usual way. Father de La Chétardye did not visit the classes
for several weeks. However, he seemed to be everywhere else in
the parish, fully justifying the remark he had made to me that
there was only one superior in the parish of Saint Sulpice. He had
a hand in everything and his competency could not be questioned. He was like a bishop in his domain and everyone respected him.

When discussing the situation with Brother Thomas one
day, I was surprised to hear the interpretation he gave to Father
de La Chétardye's attitude toward our superior.

"I went to visit Madame Voisin several days ago," Brother
Thomas told me, "to collect the monthly stipend she gives us to
help with our rent. She tells me that the Grand'Maison is up for
sale for only 45,000 pounds."

"I can't believe it. The property must be worth three times
that amount. What does Father de La Salle say?"

"He has his heart set on it. `It is the ideal place for the
Mother House of our Society,' he says, but of course we don't
have that kind of money. He says that Providence will provide.
He is going to begin a special novena of prayer this weekend to
ask Providence to inspire some rich and charitable soul to provide the money."

"And who could that charitable soul be if not Madame Voisin?" I suggested.

"You never know, Brother François. But she did say something very strange to me. She said that Father de La Chétardye succeeds in everything he puts his hand to, that he is doing an amazing job in the parish, but that he harbors one regret, that he was not inspired to found the Society of the Brothers of the Christian Schools himself, in place of our own superior, Father de La Salle. He must be a jealous man."

Madame Voisin's wise observation may have had even more meaning than she was aware of. Soon we were to have very tangible proof that the crevice separating the two men was wider and deeper than we had ever imagined.

The solemn novena started the following Saturday morning after an inspiring exhortation by Father de La Salle. All the Brothers from Paris were present. We carried lighted candles as we marched in procession through the garden and back to the chapel, chanting the psalms and the litanies of Our Lady. We then renewed our vows in the presence of the Blessed Sacrament. Father de La Salle blessed the house and all of us, and in a final prayer, asked God that the Grand'Maison might become our permanent home and the Mother House of our young Society. It was agreed that Father de La Salle, the novices, and the Brothers living at the Grand'Maison would repeat the precession every morning during the week and that those of us in the schools would have our classes join in prayer for this special intention. The following Saturday and Sunday we would come together again for the closing ceremonies of the novena.

The fervor and the confidence of the Brothers increased each day. Father de La Salle had so inspired us during this novena that we were absolutely convinced our prayers would be heard. Nothing would have surprised us, I think, not even a messenger from heaven, nor gold pieces falling from the fruit trees in the garden, nor a visit from one of the nuns buried in the crypt to tell us who our benefactor would be. But none of this was necessary, for our community received word a few days later that a wealthy person, who had died that very week, had been inspired on his death bed to leave 50,000 pounds sterling to establish this novitiate. The sum had been deposited at the rectory in the care of Father de La Chétardye.

When Father de La Salle went to the rectory to arrange for the transfer of the money and for the purchase of the property,

Father de La Chétardye would not see him. Instead, the pastor had an assistant inform our superior that the Cardinal Archbishop, being away from Paris, had not yet been consulted in the matter. Father de La Salle was further reminded that he had no letters patent from the King to authorize such a foundation, nor did he have official ecclesiastical approbation for his Society; that the pastor alone would determine how the money was to be used, since it had been deposited with him.

One word, a simple gesture on the part of Father de La Chétardye would have sufficed to settle any question with the Cardinal Archbishop and the matter of letters patent. Instead, the pastor chose to oppose our permanent installment in the Grand'Maison. We could not imagine what his next move might be. Father de La Salle was disillusioned yet confident, but there seemed to be no way that he could intervene directly to recover the legacy.

Father de La Chétardye became more and more hostile as the weeks passed. He had lost the quarrel over our religious garb, Father de La Salle having firmly upheld the position I had taken. Now he tried to impose certain changes in our regulations, but this too failed when the Brothers refused to follow his suggestions. Having complete financial control over the five schools now functioning in his parish, over the teacher training school and the Grand'Maison, he easily convinced himself that the Brothers were completely dependent on him, that Father de La Salle held but a secondary rank and could easily be put aside. What the pastor did not know was that we ourselves had elected Father de La Salle as our superior and had promised that under no circumstances would we accept any other.

It so happened, however, that events played admirably into the hands of Father de La Chétardye at a time when Father De La Salle was away from Paris. He had gone to Chartres to fulfill his promise of sending Brothers there to teach in the charity schools of the city. Brother Michael, the director of novices at the Grand'Maison, made some very imprudent decisions. For some insignificant violations of the community regulations, he obliged two young members of the community to bare their shoulders and receive twenty strokes of the discipline. This was a penance commonly used by the Trappist monks for whom Brother Michael had great admiration, but quite unsuitable for young members of our Society.

The two novices managed to leave the Grand'Maison the next day. They went straight to the rectory, where they presented their grievances to Father de La Chétardye.

No sooner had Father de La Salle returned from Chartres than the Vicar General of the archdiocese, a priest by the name of Pirot, called on us at the Grand'Maison. He was a venerable old man in his seventies who had always been a sincere friend of our superior. It soon became evident that this was not a visit of friendship. He had come to make an investigation. Although considerable effort was made to shroud the interviews with secrecy, everyone knew that the novices were being questioned one by one in private and at considerable length. The silence imposed on us by our community regulations, especially during weekend recollections, helped to create an atmosphere of uneasiness and foreboding.

The day following Pirot's visit, Father de La Salle was informed by messenger that the Cardinal Archbishop wished to see him. We did not learn the result of the interview until the following Sunday, the first of Advent.

Father de La Salle called all the Brothers of Paris to the Grand'Maison. He asked the novices to decorate the assembly room. A platform had been placed in front with two armchairs on it. The general commotion aroused the curiosity of the Brothers. Who was to be so singularly honored in our home? Even the Cardinal himself had always been received simply and without ceremony.

The morning passed uneventfully. In his ordinary calm fashion, Father de La Salle spoke to us about the Sunday Gospel.

"There shall be signs in the sun and the moon and the stars," he said, quoting the sacred text. "And on the earth distress of nations—men withering away for fear and expectation of what shall come upon them."

His commentary had been eloquent. Confidence in divine Providence, even when God's hand seems to strike the hardest, was Father de La Salle's favorite theme and he developed it impressively.

Afternoon came. The degree of expectation and curiosity reached a climax when a clanging of the bell called us to the assembly hall. The novices, the postulants, all the Brothers from Paris were in their places. I chose to remain in the back of the room near the corner window, where I could command a good view of the street below.

I had been watching only a few minutes when a carriage drove up and stopped in front of the house. The Vicar General, Father Pirot, alighted, accompanied by a young priest. Father de La Salle met them himself and escorted them to the assembly room. Our superior introduced the visitors. The young priest was Father Bricot, whom Father de La Salle praised highly. The visitors took their places in the armchairs on the platform. Father de La Salle chose to sit among the Brothers.

The Vicar General began:

"God has seen fit to make use of a man of great virtue to found the very important work of the Christian Schools. Father de La Salle gave up his fortune and his position as Canon of the Cathedral of Reims to do this work. He has undergone great trials and has sacrificed himself completely on your behalf. You have every reason to be grateful to him."

The Brothers were delighted with these words. Convinced that he had gained their confidence, the Vicar General turned toward Father Bricot and began to proclaim in no less eloquent language the eminent merits of this young priest. If any of the Brothers had been momentarily distracted, their attention was quickly aroused by a sudden turn in the discourse.

"Since Father Bricot is a man of such great virtue and in every way worthy of your esteem, he has been chosen as your superior. You must, therefore, be perfectly obedient to him in all things."

The Vicar General had not even finished his last sentence before everyone became aware of the meaning of this drama. A general disturbance followed. Brother Vuyart stood up and spoke above the din.

"Your Reverence, we already have a superior. It's Father de La Salle. I'm sure there is not one of us in this room who cares to have any other."

The Vicar General tried to ignore Brother Vuyart. "I am here only to fulfill the wishes of his Eminence the Cardinal Archbishop. You are bound in conscience to submit to his orders."

"Excuse me, Father," I called out. "May I ask what you mean by his orders? We have elected Father de La Salle as our superior. Perhaps his Eminence the Cardinal has not been informed or perhaps he has been misinformed. There has surely been some mistake."

Others began asking questions and making objections in disorderly fashion. The situation was fast slipping beyond the Vicar General's control. His face reddened and his hands twitched nervously. Father Bricot seemed extremely embarrassed too, though I could see that Father de La Salle was much more mortified than either of them. I had been watching his reaction. Now, he stood up.

"Brothers, you must remain calm." We quieted down. "The whole matter needs some explanation. His Eminence has decided to send you another superior. You must submit to the Cardinal's decision."

"But we have vowed obedience to you, Father de La Salle, not to the Cardinal," I protested. "And we promised never to accept any other priest as superior."

The Vicar General intervened again. "Father Bricot is very interested in your welfare. You can be sure that he has all the virtues that you could desire in a superior. He is kind, devoted, generous."

"Father de La Salle has all these qualities," I insisted, "and many more besides. We could never find anyone to compare with him."

"There is no question of comparison here. This is an order from his Eminence. I have the decree here."

"I think Brother is right," Father Bricot said. "There must have been some mistake. I, for one, am ready to leave."

The Vicar General hesitated. Then Brother Michael, the director of novices, stood up to speak. "Your Reverence, may I explain that Father de La Salle was not at all to blame. I was the one."

"What do you mean explain?" interrupted the Vicar General angrily. He pointed a trembling finger at Brother Michael. "You are the one who caused this disturbance in the first place."

"Please, your Reverence," Father de La Salle begged. "I appointed Brother Michael as director of novices. The responsibility is all mine. I shall go to the Cardinal to apologize for all that has happened. The Brothers will submit in time, I am sure."

At this point, Father Bricot rose to leave and was followed reluctantly by the Vicar General. Even as Father de La Salle accompanied them to the door, promising to do everything in his power to get the Brothers to submit, one of the Brothers called after them in a loud voice:

"If a new superior is sent here, then he had better bring a new community along with him. We will leave the house with Father de La Salle."

A foreboding stillness descended on the Grand'Maison. Father de La Salle disappeared from the scene. Brother Michael sent the novices off to the chapel and retired to his room. Most of the other Brothers left quietly for the schools in the city. Evening came all too slowly to shroud the scene of the day's catastrophe in somber shadows.

Morning dawned and life at the Grand'Maison resumed its normal course. Father de La Salle asked me to accompany him to the Cardinal's palace. He wanted to apologize for what he called our insubordinate conduct. It seemed strange that we were ushered in almost immediately. When his Eminence asked our superior to come closer to his desk, I remained near the door.

"Monsieur de La Salle, I am indeed surprised to see you here," the Cardinal said. "You are no longer the superior of the Brothers. I have seen to your replacement. But now, since your disciples refuse to accept my decision, I feel obliged to take even more severe measures."

"I beseech your Eminence to excuse the conduct of the Brothers. It is all my fault."

"Excuse them! Your choice of words is hardly appropriate. Unless they submit, the Cardinal Archbishop of Paris can do without their services."

"I shall persuade them to submit, your Eminence."

"You have never learned to practice the virtue of obedience yourself. How do you pretend to teach it to others? You are not submissive to ecclesiastical authority. You have refused to allow priests in your order."

" The Brothers are educators, not priests. They would not have time to be both," Father de La Salle said simply.

"Fine words for a man who has supposedly devoted his life to order and discipline! Do you realize that wherever you go you stir up trouble?"

"As you say, your Eminence."

"You want to reform everything. You have no respect for established custom or for practices that have existed for centuries. Why can't you let well enough alone?"

"Your Eminence, if we do not change things that need to be changed, then someone with no regard for the poor will do it and the poor will suffer."

"It's not a question of the poor, Monsieur de La Salle; the poor will always be with us. It's a question of principle. Our society and the Church, too, have their own establishment which must be respected."

"I am not a stranger to what you are saying, your Eminence. My father was a magistrate in the establishment you speak of. As his oldest son, I learned early from him that the establishment does indeed exist, but may not be as well founded as you presume. I have also learned from the children in our schools that class distinction does not exist among them. And does not Jesus say that unless we become as little children, we shall not enter into his kingdom?"

"That is enough, Monsieur de La Salle. You yourself are a member of the aristocracy. How can you preach such doctrine? You are a stubborn man. Your presence in Paris can only continue to cause trouble. We have, therefore, felt obliged to draw up a decree of banishment. It is here on my desk. What do you have to say?"

"Nothing, your Eminence. As long as the Brothers' work for the poor goes on, it does not matter where I am. I can find God anywhere. When am I to leave?"

"From this episcopal palace, when you wish. From the city and the archdiocese of Paris, you will be informed in good time. Au revoir, Monsieur de La Salle."

I had listened, totally stunned at the Cardinal's demeanor. Father de La Salle joined me at the door and we left in silence; no one showed us out. As we emerged from the building, we met the Vicar General hurrying through the gate.

"The Brothers at the Grand'Maison told me I might find you here, Father," he said, "but I fear I am too late. I had hoped to spare you another unpleasant meeting with his Eminence."

"That is very kind of you, Father Pirot."

"I saw the Cardinal last evening, but I was unable to convince him that this whole matter has been a terrible mistake. He is resolved to make you leave Paris if the Brothers do not submit promptly."

"He has just told me so."

"I realize your position, Father. For my own part, I sincerely admire the devotedness and attachment of the Brothers to you. Indeed, if there were such union in all the religious communities of Paris, the Church would be spared many a problem."

This compliment embarrassed Father de La Salle. "As for being exiled, he said, "you may inform his Eminence that I am prepared to go wherever he might care to send me."

"Let's not talk about exile. As long as the Cardinal has not sent a written decree of banishment, there is still hope."

With this, the Vicar General left. It was good to know that we still had a friend in him, despite what had happened the day before.

After this visit, Father de La Salle secluded himself in his room and was seen only at the community prayers and Mass. We knew that he would no longer act as superior. It was up to us, then, to face the predicament as well as we could. We decided that we would spend the next day and night in prayer and fasting. If the Cardinal did not change his mind within the week, we resolved to close our schools and leave Paris.

Word of our plan soon reached the ears of Father de La Chétardye. He had not been seen on the premises once during the past few days, although we well knew that he was actually behind all this trouble. He wanted to have direct control over the Brothers and there was no way to achieve his purpose without having Father de La Salle replaced. Now he came to the house himself to see our superior.

"You must prevent the withdrawal of the Brothers," he demanded.

"You forget, Father, that I am no longer the superior of the Brothers and consequently have no right to exercise any authority over them."

"But what will become of the schools? Would you turn all those children back into the street?"

"His Eminence has said that he would provide."

"But I can't do without the Brothers. Can't you see that there is no one else in Paris able to replace them?"

"I have tried everything possible. Perhaps you may succeed where I have failed."

Exasperated, Father de La Chétardye rushed off to the Cardinal's residence. He finally persuaded his Eminence not to send the decree of banishment. A compromise was agreed upon. His Eminence named an ecclesiastical superior to visit the Grand'Maison once a month. It was understood that this visitor would not interfere with the internal government of the Society. His visit would be one of civility and nothing more. He came to the house, in fact, only once and felt so utterly out of place that he never returned. As for Father de La Chétardye, though he had succeeded in keeping the Brothers in his parish, he remained cold and unfriendly toward Father de La Salle.

Not all was sad for our Society, however. It was about this time that a fine young man by the name of Joseph Truffet came to the Grand'Maison to join us. He was from Douai in the north and had finished his studies at the Jesuit college there. His father was a schoolteacher. We were curious to know why he had chosen our Society. There were no Brothers in Douai and the Jesuits themselves were teachers. I learned that he had first thought about becoming a priest and had studied philosophy and theology, but later, at the age of twenty-five, he decided to enter the monastery of La Trappe, some forty miles southwest of Paris. Father de Rancé, who was still superior there, counseled him against the severe vocation of the Trappist monk because of his health. It was there that he learned about Father de La Salle and the Brothers.

Joseph Truffet became Brother Barthélemy when he received the Brothers' robe from the hands of Father de La Salle. Our superior discovered at once that this young man was of extraordinary caliber, learned, intelligent, humble, and profoundly religious. He was, in fact, to play an important role in the future of our Society.

Brother Michael was still director of novices at this time. We did not know what to expect from him after all the trouble we had been through with the pastor and the Cardinal on account of him. Then one morning it was remarked that he and another Brother were nowhere to be found. They had totally disappeared from the Grand'Maison. A little investigation in the garden showed that during the night they had made use of a ladder to scale the wall and get access to the street beyond. It was three or four days later that Father de La Salle received a message from the superior at the Trappist Monastery saying that the two Brothers were seeking admission there. Brother Michael supposedly wanted to do penance for all the trouble he had caused. He had convinced one of the novices to go along with him.

By return messenger, Father de La Salle asked the Abbot to send the two Brothers back to the Grand'Maison, which he promptly did. The novice did not remain in the community much longer, attracted as he was by a way of life much more secluded and rigorous than ours, but he never became a Trappist either. Brother Michael asked to resign as director of novices and was sent to teach school in Chartres.

13

BUSINESS IS BUSINESS and Parisian landowners at the turn of the century, when their "Sun King" was reveling in all his glory at Versailles, believed that maxim just as do money changers of any age. Consequently, it did not take the owners of the Grand'Maison long to come to the conclusion that our spacious mansion was not haunted at all. Certainly no complaints had been filed, and to all appearances the haunting spirits of earlier days had vacated the premises. The proprietors had been willing to rent the house for a nominal price when suspicion and superstition ran against them; but, now that the ghostly disturbances had subsided and people stopped spreading rumors, it became self-evident that there was more money to be made with this valuable piece of property than the Brothers could ever pay.

After the great deception caused by the loss of the legacy that would have enabled us to become owners of the Grand'Maison, Father de La Salle found himself in a very serious dilemma. It was not exactly a surprise when the owners came to notify him that the place had been sold. He was given two weeks to vacate the premises. But where was he to go? Could he find a pastor somewhere in Paris who would accept him and the novices into his parish? When the two weeks were up and he still had not found a suitable place to establish his novitiate, nor had the new owner found tenants to replace the Brothers, Father de La Salle asked to be allowed to remain at the Grand'Maison for a time. The request was granted very graciously and even rent free under the condition that the Brothers would not take advantage of this prolongation to harvest the fruit in the garden. A caretaker, his wife, and their little baby were to live in the house to see that the Brothers respected the rights of the owner. This was a serious but unavoidable inconvenience to the Brothers and an intrusion on their privacy.

It was then and during the next seven weeks during which we remained at the Grand'Maison, that very strange things began to happen. The novices whispered that the ghost of an old nun buried in the crypt was wandering about the premises at night. Two of the Brothers even claimed that she had appeared to them. Her principal task, however, seemed to be to frighten the caretaker and his wife out of the house and to convince the new owner that the property was destined to be a convent or a monastery and nothing else. Though the spirits succeeded in chasing the caretaker out of the main building without too much opposition, and to the great relief of the community, they could not seem to convince the proprietor to keep the Brothers on the premises indefinitely, rent free. And so it was that we left the Grand'Maison during the summer vacation of 1703.

Father de La Salle got a warm welcome and found a real friend when he visited the pastor of St. Paul's parish and asked authorization to establish his novitiate there. He had found a building on Charonne Street that seemed adequate. It was located near the convent of the Sisters of the Holy Cross, where he could say Mass every morning for our community. These good nuns became our principal benefactors in Paris at a time when practically no help was coming from Father de La Chétardye. The community consisted of the principal Brothers, those in charge of special services like Brother Thomas, Brother Jean Jacquot, Brother Antoine, Brother Dominic Sellier, who had been directing the school at the Grand'Maison, and Brother Barthélemy, whom Father de La Salle was preparing to be the director of novices. Several younger Brothers came along to be employed in the charity school that was to be opened.

The pastor also allowed Father de La Salle to open a Sunday School for young men, age 14 to 20, manual laborers or apprentices for the most part, who needed to complete their schooling. They were divided into several classes according to age and ability. The most backward were instructed in reading and writing.

The others received lessons in arithmetic and drawing or what-ever they needed to develop their personal skills. Everyone fol-lowed the religion classes.

The great advantage of the Sunday School, in addition to keeping these young men from getting into trouble with the law or from idling in the streets or taverns, was to give them a taste for the Arts, a motive for self-development and a way to establish themselves little by little in society. At the same time they were taught to lead Christian lives. Father de La Salle turned away no one who applied for the Sunday School and neither would he ac-cept any payment for the instruction imparted. The only re-quirement for admission was a promise of good will and acceptance of the measures for good order required for everyone. This was not difficult because Father de La Salle had a way of making his authority not only acceptable but appreciated. The school quickly made a name for itself, but also excited the jeal-ousy of the Writing Masters.

The transfer of the central community of our Society from the Grand'Maison to Charonne Street, the antipathy of Father de La Chétardye that had brought it about, and the misconduct of Brother Michael, had taken their toll on our numbers. Some Brothers, appalled at the animosity that seemed to assail our Society on all sides, chose to look for a more comfortable exis-tence elsewhere.

It so happened at this time that Brother Barthélemy took very ill. His health had never been good but now his condition became alarming. He developed a kind of scrofula or tuberculo-sis of the bones and glands which caused sores to break out on his neck and arms. At the same time he received word that his fa-ther had passed away and that the authorities of his native vil-lage were keeping the post of schoolteacher open for him with the same salary that his father had received. Some Brothers of the community, fearing that his disease could be contagious, tried to persuade him to leave the Society and accept the teaching job that was being offered to him. Brother Barthélemy resisted; he wanted to live and die as a Brother. The doctor who examined him confirmed that a cure was very problematical.

Some of the Brothers then took up the matter with Father de La Salle whose custom it was to share his authority with the prin-cipal Brothers of the Society and to spend a great deal of time in prayer before making important decisions. He often used to say: "One must pray very much to know God's will and even more to obtain his help to accomplish it."

Finally, realizing that the principal Brothers were determined to have Brother Barthélemy leave the Society, since he might always be a handicap and could endanger the health of other Brothers, Father de La Salle gave in to their wishes. He asked Brother Thomas to help Brother Barthélemy prepare for his departure early the next morning. I don't think that our superior, in the depths of his heart, really accepted the idea of sending him away. He held Brother Barthélemy in very great esteem as did we all, and further, he had always been very patient in trying to persuade even wayward Brothers to remain in the Society and to change their ways. If it had not been for this contagious disease, there would have been no opposition to Brother Barthélemy's presence in the community. Besides, Father de La Salle was preparing him, it seemed, to become the director of novices to replace Brother Michael who had already gone to Chartres.

When, the following morning, Brother Thomas went to Father de La Salle's room for the keys to open the gate, he was startled to discover that our superior had spent the night in prayer. After midnight, he had had a long talk with Brother Barthélemy. Finding him entirely submissive to the will of God as expressed by the decision of the Brothers, but still willing to sacrifice the teaching offer that had been made to him by his native villagers, Father de La Salle decided not to send him away after all.

Our superior found the means to confide Brother Barthélemy to the care of a specialist. A surgeon was called in to perform several very painful operations. Together, the two doctors succeeded in curing him. Brother Barthélemy's health remained poor after this treatment but all danger of contagion had been eliminated and everyone was happy that he had not been sent away. Some months later, Father de La Salle named him the director of novices.

In the parish where the novitiate, the Sunday school, and the charity school were located, there were already several schools conducted by our old rivals, the Writing Masters. They had very few pupils compared with the large numbers that flocked to our schools, and it vexed them to no end to see that our teaching was entirely gratuitous. Since the law gave them the exclusive right to charge a fee for the teaching of writing, it was little wonder that they did everything in their power to render our situation impossible. The growing popularity of our schools was more than they could endure. A showdown, sooner or later, seemed inevitable.

When the Writing Masters tried to close the school on Princess Street in 1690, Father de La Salle had taken the matter to court and had won the case. Now, they were determined to win. Either our lawyer was incapable or our enemies had their claims too well prepared, because everything went wrong. Father de La Salle himself received a summons to appear at police headquarters.

The pastor of the parish, maintaining that he had a perfect right to conduct a free school in his parish and to choose the teachers he wished, advised Father de La Salle to ignore the summons. To our surprise it was not repeated, but the exasperated Writing Masters, seeing that they could not win their point any other way, took the law into their own hands. Late one evening, they broke into the school, destroyed benches and tables, tore maps and charts from the walls, threw everything into the yard to be burned.

Fighting started in the street when angry parents tried to chase the vandals off the premises. The Writing Masters' pay school in that same part of town would certainly have been destroyed in retaliation had not several officers of the law appeared on the scene to reestablish order. The next morning, the same officers returned to board up the doors and windows of our building while parents, pupils and Brothers looked on helplessly. A week later, the Sunday School suffered the same fate.

Thus, deprived of a home, and faced with the grim prospect of a none-too-friendly welcome by Father de La Chétardye on Princess Street, Father de La Salle decided to move the novitiate to the parish of Saint Hippolytus, where Brother Nicolas Vuyart was directing a training college.

Providence seemed to be calling us there for another reason as well. The pastor of that parish had died some months before and had left a very large sum of money for the upkeep of the training college. Since Father de La Salle was not actually working there, the pastor had bequeathed the money to Brother Vuyart for this purpose. It was a considerable sum and only recently had the full amount come into Vuyart's hands. A community at Saint Hippolytus could well support the presence of the novitiate. The situation would be similar to that on New Street in Reims in 1687.

The idea of participating in the formation of these future teachers pleased me. Since I had been asked to help the novices move to their new home, I was happy to go with Father de La Salle one morning to make arrangements with Brother Vuyart.

I recognized the young man who opened the door.

"Good morning, Father de La Salle," he said. "Good morning, Jacques. You are Jacques Delanot, aren't you? I thought I recognized you."

Father de La Salle said good morning and asked to see Brother Nicolas.

"If you mean Monsieur Vuyart," the young man answered, "he is very busy at the moment. I'm sure he will see you as soon as possible. I'll let him know that you are here."

We waited an uncomfortably long time. When the door finally opened, the figure standing there, tall and domineering, was not wearing the Brother's robe but the silk waistcoat and knee-breeches of the wealthy. The long flaxen wig added a tint of arrogance.

"Good morning, Father de La Salle," Vuyart said, bowing slightly. "Good morning to you, too, Brother François."

"Brother Nicolas, how is it that . . . ," Father de La Salle stumbled over his own words.

"I think I understand, Monsieur. You find my attire strange. Perhaps I did forget to inform you. I am no longer a member of the Society of the Christian Brothers. I have chosen to conduct the training college in an entirely different way. A number of things have changed. I hope you will be able to understand. You so like to change things yourself."

"It is quite possible that our ideas differ concerning the method of training teachers, Brother Nicolas, but surely that cannot interfere with your vocation."

"My vocation is my business. I have already made up my mind about that. If there is nothing else you would like to discuss. . . ."

"Just a moment," I interrupted, unable to hold back my anger any longer. "I have a few things to say to you, Vuyart. You have no right to speak to Father de La Salle like this. Everything you have you owe to him. You betrayed him once in Reims and he forgave you, but this is much more serious. I cannot believe that you have actually stolen the money that the pastor left to this training college."

"I didn't steal it. It was left to me."

"Do you remember the solemn promise you made in the presence of Father de La Salle and all of us?"

"I've never been particularly fond of poverty. And as for that robe you are wearing, it has become a laughing-stock of the city! Besides, I have no time for sentimentality. Let us forget the past.

The future is rich with promise. So, if you desire nothing else in particular, I would prefer to return to my work."

The door of the parlor closed abruptly. Nicolas Vuyart was gone.

With heavy hearts, we walked back to Princess Street, not knowing where else to go. I was angry at Vuyart for his treachery, angry at the Writing Masters for their vandalism and angry at myself for not being able to do anything about it.

14

Our society had never been closer to ruin than during that first decade of the new century. Our Founder was an outcast. The ecclesiastical hierarchy no longer considered him the superior of the Society he had founded. The cardinal had never retracted the decree that had deposed him and Father de La Chétardye considered this ample justification for his interference in our affairs.

Nicolas Vuyart, who with Father de La Salle and Brother Gabriel Drolin had solemnly vowed fidelity to the Society, had deserted. It had taken him only a short time to squander the money that he had inherited so unjustly. Father de La Salle had taken every means in his power to bring him back to the Society, but all his efforts, prayers, letters, and subsequent interviews had been to no avail. Our superior never quite got over the sadness of this desertion. He considered himself largely responsible, saying that we should have listened to him and chosen someone more competent to be the superior of the community. He often spoke of Brother Gabriel Drolin, the other cornerstone of the Society, who was far away in Rome, directing a small school there. Would he become discouraged because of the long separation? Would he, too, forget the promise he had made?

Very serious problems remained to be faced in the capital if we were to survive at all. Residence at the training school now being completely out of the question, we returned once more, a weary and dejected little group, to our old home on Princess Street. Here, during several months, misfortune followed misfortune. Several other Brothers followed Vuyart in leaving the Society. An epidemic in Chartres carried off four more Brothers in a few weeks. Brother Michael was one of them. Finally, proud of their recent victories, the Writing Masters renewed their attacks on the schools in our parish. This time success crowned their efforts. They pillaged the school on Princess Street mercilessly, carrying away everything in the place, even the furniture. Father de La Chétardye, the only one who could have defended us and who had the legal right to do so, remained indifferent. Instead, he tried by every means to bend the will of our superior to his way of thinking. He even diminished our food supplies until we were reduced to the last extremity.

Fortunately, in the midst of this new onslaught, a priest from Saint Roch's parish asked Father de La Salle to open a school there. Our superior saw in this invitation the work of Providence. The Writing Masters were not yet active in that section of the city because of the extreme poverty of its inhabitants. Our superior and four Brothers were therefore able to settle there quietly, all their needs taken care of by the pastor. The school flourished immediately. Then a petition came to open a school in Rouen. Since work in Paris had now become next to impossible, Father de La Salle gladly accepted this offer as well. Withdrawing the Brothers from Paris might perhaps calm the tempest.

The Sunday following the sacking of the last of our schools in the parish of Saint Sulpice, Brother Paul Narra and those who still remained on Princess Street set out in the early morning to meet Father de La Salle and several other Brothers. We had not said a word to Father de La Chétardye about our departure. It had been decided that we would leave Paris as secretly as possible. Only two Brothers were to remain in the city, at Saint Roch's. The pastor wanted them to stay at all costs.

What a difference, now in 1705, from the time when I had first journeyed from Paris to Rouen almost 35 years before. Then I had been running away from school. Now, I was actually coming to Rouen to teach! Then, the love of adventure had been my motive. Now, duty called—duty made all the more pleasant by the prospect it offered of revisiting those places linked to the fondest memories of my boyhood: those months in the Maillefer mansion, the mysterious death of the old beggar, that first encounter with Monsieur Nyel.

On reaching the city, Father de La Salle led us immediately to the churchyard of Saint Maclou to say a prayer at the tomb of Adrian Nyel, who had died almost 20 years before. I thanked God for having used this man to lead me to Father de La Salle.

Conditions in Rouen were now even more deplorable than they had been in 1672. The work of Adrian Nyel had been completely neglected after his death. The group of teachers that he had tried to establish in Rouen had now been disbanded. We were called in by the town magistrates to replace them.

We were lodged in the public hospital, taught class eight hours every day, took care of the sick during the time we were not in the classroom and, in addition, devoted time to Mass and prayer. This proved to be a burdensome schedule, but weeks passed before our superior could make any arrangements to ease the situation.

Eventually, thanks to gifts from friends, Father de La Salle was able to purchase a large property across the river. It was called Saint Yon. From then on, as we no longer lived in the public hospital, we were not responsible for the sick lodged there. We continued to teach classes, walking each day to the school. Saint Yon soon became the center of our Society. Here Father de La Salle opened the novitiate once more. He also opened a boarding school and a reform school.

We had been in Rouen for only a few weeks when word came from Paris that the parents of our former pupils were clamoring for our return. At first the parishioners had imagined that some extraordinary holidays had been given, but when they realized that we had left the parish and the schools for good, they exerted all the pressure they could on Father de La Chétardye to send for us. He was finally obliged to write to our superior.

"I beg you to forget the unfortunate events that have taken place and to send the Brothers back to us. I am besieged day and night by the pleading cries of these poor people who are left without hope. On my part, I assure you that the Brothers you may deign to send us will be suitably lodged and adequately paid, and I shall do everything in my power to protect them against the Writing Masters."

All the poor schools of Rouen had been offered to Father de La Salle. He had real friends in the person of the bishop and the clergy of Rouen and prospects looked bright for recruiting new teachers there. In view of all this, it would only have been reasonable to ignore the pleas of Father de La Chétardye. After all, the pastor of Saint Sulpice had already caused the Brothers enough trouble. Instead, Father de La Salle, who had always tried to adapt his own feelings to the needs of the poor children in our schools, without demanding more of Father de La Chétardye, agreed to send six of us back to the capital.

Father de La Salle did not look on things from a personal point of view. I knew him well enough to realize that his character was far too noble to take petty grievances into consideration and his heart far too big to limit his labor of love to one place or another. He wanted to win the whole world to God. There was no limit to his zeal. Besides, he had not forgotten the hundreds of poor children he had been obliged to abandon by withdrawing the Brothers from the Paris schools. Gladly would he send their teachers back to them.

Father de La Chétardye received us well enough and seemed determined to safeguard us against any future trouble. Nevertheless, he again insisted on the appointment of an ecclesiastical superior who would visit the house monthly. We began to fear that his obstinacy in this matter might still have serious consequences, despite the written agreement made at the Grand'Maison. As long as Father de La Salle remained away, however, our relationship with Father de La Chétardye was satisfactory. Brother Thomas always managed to stay on good terms with him. It was, in fact, Brother Thomas's good relationship with Father de La Chétardye that saved us on many occasions.

Our first preoccupation on returning to Paris was to find suitable lodging. The living quarters above the classrooms on Princess Street were not only noisy and unhealthy but totally unsuitable for a religious community. Brother Thomas found a place on La Barouillère Street somewhat similar to the Grand'Maison, though not as large, with enclosed garden and courtyard and two important buildings. Father de La Salle came, in secret, to visit the house. He was delighted with it but didn't want to come forward himself to apply for a lease. He wanted to keep a certain distance from Father de La Chétardye. He therefore encouraged Brother Thomas to use all his personal diplomacy to get the pastor's approval and a promise that he would pay the rent. Everything went smoothly. To our great satisfaction, we were able to move into our new residence within the month.

Father de La Chétardye seemed particularly pleased on this occasion to deal with Brother Thomas and the other Brothers directly. He could do so now that the schools in his parish had reopened and Father de La Salle was nowhere to be seen. When our superior did come to Paris, he did so discreetly and remained in Saint Roch's parish so as not to give the pastor an occasion to be disagreeable. The four schools were within walking distance from our new residence. Those on St. Placid and Princess Streets were the closest; those on Du Bac and Fossez Monsieur le Prince, somewhat farther. We walked to and from our particular schools each morning and evening.

We had not been long back to work in the parish when war broke out again with the Writing Masters. Seeing that their pillaging of the schools had not brought about a real change after all, and that we were back at work just as before, they began their disturbances again with a vengeance. In the absence of Father de La Salle they tried to intimidate us by repeated threats of lawsuits, fines, and even imprisonment. They harassed us in the streets on every possible occasion. When all this failed, they demanded and obtained a court injunction forbidding us to accept in our classes any children whose parents were not publicly listed as paupers. But who was to draw the line of distinction? Just where would the boundaries be?

When the Brothers of the area assembled to tell Father de La Salle of this latest development, he was indignant. He had come back to Paris for a few days and had stopped in to see us, believing that Father de La Chétardye had kept his promise and that things were going smoothly. He found it hard to believe all the unpleasant things we had to tell him about the Writing Masters and about the pastor.

"We can never accept this injunction," he said. "It would set limits even to charity. It is contrary to the very Gospel principle on which the Christian schools are founded. I will do everything in my power to oppose it and I ask you to do the same."

"But the pastor seems to have given his approval," I said. "He has named a priest who is supposed to judge the children's level of poverty. He's forever coming into the classes to ask embarrassing questions. He even brings the Writing Masters to the school, or sometimes there is an officer of the law with him. They force some of the boys out of the classroom or they stand in the street and prevent others from entering. Some of the parents, even the poorest, don't want to send their children to school any longer, if they have to submit to this humiliation. What are we going to do, Father?"

Before answering my question, Father de La Salle looked around the assembly, registering the reactions on all our faces. The four of us from the Princess Street school were sitting

together, Brother Simeon Pajot next to me. He and I had been together for some years. He was a real expert at weaving and Father
de La Salle had put him in charge of the shop. Brother Théodore
Sellier was one of the four brothers from Villiers-Le-Bel. Brother
Paul Narra had become a real artist besides being an excellent
teacher.

To the right of us sat Brother Ponce Thiseux with his helper
Brother Alexis Jourdain from the school on St. Placid Street. To
the left were Brother Clément Gatelet and Marc Morel from the
school on Du Bac Street. In front of them, my good friend Brother Thomas was sitting with the two Brothers from the school on
Fossez-Monsieur-le-Prince Street, Joseph Le Roux and Charles
Michel. These were all men deeply concerned about what was
happening to our Society in Paris. Perhaps the most concerned
was my own little community on Princess Street, because we
were under the direct eye of Father de La Chétardye, spending
most of our day in the shadow of the parish rectory.

Father de La Salle began to speak.

"Before I answer your question, Brother François, I would
like to hear from the other Brothers. What do you have to say,
Brother Ponce?"

"Our school on St. Placid Street is no exception to what
Brother François said. I for one am disgusted and wearied by
these unrelenting inspections. I prefer to teach somewhere else. I
think we should close the schools."

"Ours is already closed, as of today." It was Brother Joseph
Le Roux who had spoken out. Everyone looked at him, surprised.
He was the director of the school on Fossez-Monsieur-le-Prince
Street.

"Yes," he continued, "but it was not I who closed it. Father
de La Chétardye came this morning. He said the complaints of
the Writing Masters were becoming too violent. He thought that
closing one of the schools would appease their anger. He said he
was sorry it had to be mine but could do nothing about it. I don't
think he is sorry. Excuse me, Father de La Salle, but I think he
may even be backing those vandals. I am ready to leave Paris. I'll
go anywhere you wish to send me."

"And you, Brother Clément, what do you have to say?"

"I have little to add. Enough has been said and it is all true.
The ultimate goal of the Writing Masters is to chase us from
Paris. They don't want us, or you, here any longer. I, for one, pre-
fer to go of my own accord."

Brother Siméon, who was sitting next to me, jumped to his feet. "I don't want to leave Paris," he shouted angrily. "If we do close the schools, I can still keep the weaving shop open. The Writing Masters have nothing to say about that. Marcel Potier wouldn't like the idea, nor the old man Rafrond, either, but I can get along with Father de La Chétardye, I think, and the shop is helping a lot of youngsters in the parish."

No one said anything for a few moments. It was as if a blast of wind had shaken the building and everyone was waiting for the trembling to cease. "Was there a Brother in the room who could possibly take sides with the pastor?" I asked myself. "Was he in my own community?"

Father de La Salle remained silent for a moment. Then he said:

"Thank you, Brothers, for expressing your opinions so frankly. I will spend the night here. If any of you have something further to say and wish to say it more privately, do not hesitate to come and see me. We will celebrate the Sunday Eucharist together tomorrow and, God willing, we will find a solution to this problem. Let us remember that we are in God's holy presence. Let us pray silently, each in his own heart, that we come to know and do God's holy will."

Night settled over Paris. Sleep came in fleeting moments. Was this the end of our Society's presence in the capital? If so, it would be the end, too, of one of Father de La Salle's dreams. He had wanted the headquarters of the Society to be in Paris where he might eventually obtain the official state and church approbation he needed so desperately to defend himself in situations like the present one. My troubled memory returned often during the night to the meeting we had just had. Would Brother Siméon remain faithful, even if Father de La Salle decided to close the weaving shop as well as the schools? Just how close was he to Father de La Chétardye?

At our community morning prayer, Father de La Salle did not seem disturbed or tired, although he had probably not gone to bed at all. He told us very simply to prepare for our departure. We were all to leave Paris that very day, except Brother Thomas, who was to stay on as discreetly as possible, keeping an eye on our home and preparing himself for any eventuality.

We would simply disappear from the capital, two by two, according to Father de La Salle's instructions, at different hours of the day, quietly and unobserved for the most part. Six of us would go to Chartres, my community, and the two Brothers from the school that had already been closed. We could reach there before nightfall. The other four set out for Rouen. They would stop overnight at the rectory in a small village where Father de La Salle had a priest friend. Our superior, too, would return to Rouen sometime during the week. It did seem that Rouen would be the real center of our Society after all.

Our schools in Paris remained shut the next day. Nobody knew why or what had become of us. As the weeks passed, all sorts of rumors spread throughout the parish. Fear lest the closing of the schools might last indefinitely caused great turmoil. Children began running wild in the streets. Disgruntled parents stormed the rectory, clamoring for an interview with Father de La Chétardye. Those lucky enough to see him did not hide their displeasure over our departure. They told him how impossible it was for them to give their children the instruction and education they needed or to send them to classes conducted by teachers who had to be paid for their services. The pastor knew full well that he had it in his power to put an end to the struggle between us and the Writing Masters. The charity schools were totally under his control. Never did he understand better the need his parish had of us, the good we were doing, the services we rendered, and the advantage religion drew from our presence in the city. He had no alternative but to call the Brothers back to the schools once more.

15

ALMOST THREE MONTHS passed nevertheless, before our superior heard from Father de La Chétardye. The pastor requested that the Brothers return to the parish schools, promising as he had done before to insure their protection, but this was not enough guarantee for Father de La Salle. He insisted on obtaining a notarized document which alone could assure the Brothers legal protection. He requested this of Father de La Chétardye at the risk of incurring his displeasure once more. The pastor did not refuse. He was bent on having the Brothers back in the parish and he knew very well that his own popularity was now linked to the success of the charity schools. He could use other means to settle his personal differences with Father de La Salle. Therefore, he called a meeting of the main officers of the Writing Masters' Guild. A document was drawn up in their presence and certified by two notaries.

This act stated that it was he, De La Chétardye, who had commissioned the Brothers (they were named individually) to teach in the charity schools of the parish; that John Baptist de La Salle, priest and Doctor in Theology, had been most regrettably interfered with in that regard by the Writing Masters, since he had employed his disciples in the work only by De La Chétardye's orders, at his expense, and in conformity with his directions; that he, the parish priest, had merely followed the example of his predecessors who had called De La Salle to Paris with his Brothers to teach the poor children of the parish; that the rent on the classroom building, as well as on the lodgings of the teachers, was paid by the parish priest himself; and finally, that it was he who had always provided the Brothers whose names appeared in the document with food and lodging; and, consequently, that these Brothers were to be allowed to continue their work freely and without interference on the part of the Writing Masters; for which purpose the present document was being drawn up, so that all concerned might take note of it and be guided by it.

Father de La Salle received a copy of the document some days later. He was satisfied with it and decided to make arrangements for our return to Paris. The pastor chose not to reopen the school on Fossez-Monsieur-le-Prince Street as a kind of compromise measure with the Writing Masters.

Father de La Salle's firmness in dealing with Father de La Chétardye and the Writing Masters put an effective restraint on the animosity of our rivals. The schools reopened and functioned normally once more to everyone's satisfaction. But there was something deeper to the conflict between Father de La Chétardye and Father de La Salle and it kept coming to the front. The pastor just did not recognize the authority of Father de La Salle over us. He wanted that authority himself. Proof of this became evident very soon after our return to Paris.

Our Superior went to the rectory to pay Father de La Chétardye a courtesy visit. He wanted to thank him for settling the quarrel with the Writing Masters and he sincerely hoped, at the same time, to iron out the differences that still existed between him and the pastor. He fully recognized that he needed the pastor just as much as the pastor needed the Brothers. His efforts proved to be of no avail. Not only was he received ungraciously, but Father de La Chétardye informed him that from then on he would pay the Brothers' salary with State-issued paper money. He well knew that we were without food.

When Brother Thomas heard the news, he was outraged.

"There is nothing, absolutely nothing, I can buy with that kind of money," he said. "It is highly suspect throughout the country and totally useless in the hands of priests and religious. I have tried it before. No butcher or baker would accept it, nor anyone else for that matter. At this point, there is no food in the house, Father de La Salle. I'm sorry. I've done all I could."

"Give me the notes, Brother Thomas. I'll try to find someone to exchange them for us." Father de La Salle took the notes and left the house.

We sat silently around the empty table. Brother Siméon was the most despondent of all but not the first to speak. It was Brother Paul Narra who stood up. I had never before seen him speak out at our meetings.

"I have some paintings that I use for models in the art classes at Sunday school," he said. "I could sell them, if you'll let me, Brother Thomas. It might help a little."

"I don't think Father de La Salle would object. Every little bit will help. Take Brother Marc with you and God bless your endeavors."

Minutes later the two of them left. Brother Paul had several canvasses tucked under his arm, partially hidden by the cape he had thrown casually over his shoulders, his tricorn hat in hand. He seemed as happy as I had always known him to be. I could already imagine him on the banks of the River Seine, facing the Cathedral of Notre Dame, where artists had their shops and where, I felt sure, he would find a willing buyer.

The voice of Brother Siméon brought me back from my daydreaming.

"It's a pity that we're reduced to this extremity. It's all because Father de La Salle can't get along with the pastor. I wonder sometimes if he realizes that. It's not up to me to tell him. Why don't you do it, Brother Thomas? You get along fine with both of them."

"We have discussed the matter several times, Siméon. It is not as simple as that. The pastor wants to change our regulations, he wants to govern our Society. I think he is disturbed because he was not the founder himself, in the first place. Father de La Salle will never give in. He is totally convinced that this work is the Lord's, not his. And I happen to be convinced that he is right."

"Well, if nobody else does anything about it, I'll try myself. It's absurd to continue living this way. In the meantime, there's money to be made with the weaving shop and I'm going to do my share to support the community."

Only a short time after Brother Siméon had left the house to return to the weaving shop, Father de La Salle came back. Either out of pity or out of charity or for some other motive we could not imagine, someone had done him the favor of exchanging the State notes for coin. He gave the money to Brother Thomas, who left at once to buy the food we needed so badly. Father de La Salle's ability to exchange State notes for regular currency amazed all those who heard about it. No one was more surprised than Father de La Chétardye himself, who with all his influence, could not have worked such a miracle.

When Brother Thomas had spent all this sum, Father de La Salle returned to the parish priest for the balance of the salary due. All he received was an ungracious refusal. He came away without either money or notes. He told us the sorry facts but made no comments.

I went to talk to him that night, feeling that he must be lonely indeed.

"Brother François," he confided, "I am a persona non grata in this parish and in this diocese. It is my own person that is objectionable. I am convinced of it. That is why one of the Brothers should be the superior of the Society. Father de La Chétardye has nothing against you and the other Brothers, and yet you are the victims. I feel like Jonas. I should be cast overboard so that the tempest may cease."

"Don't think about it that way, Father. Why do you torment yourself like this? We'll find a way."

"Brother François, I have thought it over and prayed. I am going to disappear for a time. I'm going to the Carmelite convent, where I'll have time to meditate. Providence is surely telling us something, but I can't seem to grasp it. I need to be away from everything for awhile and you need to be free to make your own decisions. Brother Thomas will know what to do."

We embraced. I left the room with a heavy heart.

The events that took place during the next two weeks were disconcerting. Brother Thomas and I were sitting in the parlor of our residence, a small room where the Brothers could receive visitors. I had just returned from Princess Street. We had met at the front door. Brother Thomas told me he had just come back from the rectory, where he had gone to request the remainder of the Brothers' salary. He began by telling the pastor that Father de La Salle had disappeared, and that no one knew where he was.

"I will give the Brothers everything they want," Father de La Chétardye replied. "Here is the remainder of their salaries, and I put aside 600 pounds to cover their expenses while the schools were closed. It is yours, Brother Thomas, but listen to me. You are an intelligent person and a fine religious. We have been working together and understanding each other ever since I became the pastor of Saint Sulpice. I have been unable to get along with Father de La Salle. He is a holy man but he is stubborn. Despite the marvels he has accomplished, he has now become an obstacle to the development of his Society and to the good it is doing in the parish. It is time for him to retire and leave the Society in the hands of the Brothers and of competent ecclesiastical authorities. I have chosen you, Brother Thomas, to be the superior. Will you accept that responsibility? Don't answer immediately. I know this may surprise you but we'll have time to talk it over leisurely. Father de La Salle seems to have begun to realize that his time is up. I personally know that he would like nothing better than to retire to some monastery and lead a contemplative life the rest of his days. Perhaps that is what he has already done without telling anyone. Think about this, Brother Thomas, and come and see me again in a few days, will you?"

"What do I do now, François?" Brother Thomas asked.

"I'm not surprised at what has happened, knowing that Father de La Chétardye likes you so much. You have the advantage, at least, of being able to pick up our salaries. That is something Father de La Salle can't do any more. The community won't starve to death, and that is a relief for everyone. We don't know how long Father de La Salle will stay away. When he does return, I'm sure he'll do so discreetly. In the meantime, you are really the superior here and there is no harm in letting the pastor know it. Just don't let him take it too far."

Father de La Salle returned to our community just as suddenly as he had left. We were overjoyed by his presence among us and we felt reassured that nothing could ever separate us from him. He did all he could to remain hidden but his return soon became known in the parish. He took refuge once more at the school on Charonne Street, far from the parish of Saint Sulpice, and let events take their course as if he were no longer in Paris and had given up his position as superior. This pleased Father de La Chétardye, who continued to deal directly with Brother Thomas and with me as director of the school on Princess Street.

One day that winter, Father de La Salle was returning to Saint Roch's parish after visiting some of the Brothers. The humidity of the river often caused the streets to be icy. He had crossed the bridge over the Seine and was entering the gate of the Tuileries Gardens when he slipped and fell. He had recently undergone an operation on one of his knees, and it was that same knee that struck a spike in the gateway as he fell. It penetrated deep into the flesh and bone, the shock and pain causing him to faint. At first, those who saw him lying in the snow thought that he was drunk, but, on coming closer and seeing the blood, they helped him back to the Brothers' house. He fainted again in the arms of the Brother who opened the door.

16

A WEEK AFTER THIS accident, I happened to meet a young cleric by the name of Jean-Charles Clément, whose future relationship with Father de La Salle was to have a very dramatic influence on our Society. He came to the school one day accompanied by Father de La Chétardye. The young man was wearing the long black soutane of the clergy, with an elegant bright blue sash around his waist, its tassels dangling as he walked.

"Brother François, this is Monsieur l'Abbé Clément," the Pastor said as the young man offered to shake hands with me.

"You are welcome to our school, Monsieur l'Abbé," I said. "What can I do for you?"

"I have been to visit the Brothers in Chartres. I am from the Benedictine Abbey of Saint-Calais, which is not far from there. The Brothers and Mgr. Godet des Marais, the bishop, told me about your work here. Would it be possible to visit the weaving shop? You do have a weaving shop where the boys learn the trade, don't you?"

"Of course, I'll be glad to accompany you, Monsieur l'Abbé."

"And, Brother François, could you arrange for him to meet Father de La Salle?" the Pastor added. "Monsieur Clément has an important matter to discuss with him and I am obliged to return to the rectory in a few minutes."

"I must tell you that Father de La Salle underwent surgery on his knee a few days ago and is still unable to walk. He is staying with the Brothers at our school in Saint Roch's parish. I am sure he will be pleased to see Monsieur Clément, especially if he brings news of Mgr. Godet des Marais. They were students together here at the seminary and are close friends."

"Then he must also know my superior at Saint-Calais," the young man said, "Monsieur Moustiers de Mérinville. He is the bishop's nephew. He will succeed his uncle, no doubt, as bishop of Chartres. At least, so have I been told, and, without being indiscreet, I might add that such a promotion would leave an interesting and lucrative position vacant at the Abbey. But let us get on with the visit, if you will, Brother. I am anxious to meet your superior."

We visited the weaving shop, in which Monsieur Clément took great interest. He watched the young apprentices working the looms, asked them all sorts of questions and examined with admiration the bolts of cloth ready to be taken to the market. I watched him as he moved about, asking myself what kind of business he could possibly have with Father de La Salle. His conduct intrigued me. Had he and Father de La Chetardye agreed to anything? Why had he mentioned an interesting and lucrative post soon to be vacant at the Abbey of Saint-Calais?

My curiosity only increased as I accompanied Clément to our school in Saint Roch's parish, where I was able to introduce him to our superior. To my amazement, the young cleric got on his knees in front of the couch where Father de La Salle was resting.

"Reverend Father," he said, "I have heard so many wonderful things about you and your work. Now I have the honor of meeting you. May I say . . . "

"Please, do sit down, Monsieur l'Abbé," Father de La Salle interrupted, ignoring the compliment and pointing to a chair. "Should I call you Monsieur l'Abbé? You look so young."

"People do call me Father, though I have not yet been ordained."

"Brother François tells me that you are from the Abbey of Saint-Calais and that your superior is the nephew of a good friend and old classmate of mine, the bishop of Chartres. I understand his health is failing, is that so?"

"Yes, and it is said that his nephew may succeed him sooner than most people believe. Can you imagine what that means to me?"

"I do not follow you, Monsieur l'Abbé."

"Then I will tell you, but what I say must be kept a secret for the time being. It is one of the reasons why I am here to see you, Monsieur de La Salle." The young man paused. Then looked up at me, a question in his eyes.

"I will just step outside. Please excuse me." I turned to leave.

"No, please don't leave, Brother François. Monsieur l'Abbé will surely understand that whatever is said here will remain confidential. Besides, I may need your help. There is another chair there by the desk. Please sit down." The calm manner of Father de La Salle seemed to impress the young cleric, who continued:

"It is whispered that your friend Monseigneur Godet des Marais has chosen his nephew, the Abbot of Saint-Calais, to be his coadjutor with the right of succession. When this happens, I shall be named Abbot of Saint-Calais with all the rights and privileges attached to that position. The King himself has promised my father that it will be so."

"This may be a wonderful opportunity for you, no doubt, Monsieur l'Abbé, but I fail to see how it is related to me or to the Brothers. I have always made it a point not to get involved in what goes on at Versailles. The Brothers devote their lives to teaching the children of artisans and of the poor. It is not befitting that they depart from this path."

"That is precisely the point I wish to make, Father de La Salle. I feel called to do something very special for the poor. Your example is largely responsible for that inspiration, and that is why I am here. When I am given the rich Abbey of Saint-Calais, I want to use all its revenue for good works. I want to found a school for young boys whom I will take in from the streets and keep for several years in order to educate them properly and to teach them a trade, weaving for example. Thus, as good Christians, they may earn their own living. I have already collected a considerable amount of clothing and all kinds of provisions. I will use my own personal allowance of 800 pounds to finance the project until I receive the revenue from the Abbey. I am ready to begin at once, Father. I beg you to give me two Brothers to help with the work, just as you did for your good friend, the bishop of Chartres, several years ago. And help me find a suitable lodging for them. Please don't say no, Father de La Salle."

Clément was on his knees again, pleading, and Father de La Salle was trying, with extended arms, to raise him up.

I had listened to the ardent plea of this young seminarian without missing a word. How extraordinary it seemed! For a moment, I thought I was hearing Adrian Nyel all over again, and yet there was something about the scene that struck me as strange. Was it in Clément's posture, the way he was dressed, his tone of voice, his manner?

"Monsieur l'Abbé Clément," Father de La Salle said, "I am indeed edified by what you have told me. Your motives are highly praiseworthy. But you are so young. Does your father approve of this move?"

"I have not told him, it is true. He might consider me a simpleton. My father is very ambitious. He is looking only for his own advancement at Court. If I don't carry out my project now, I may never do it. I may lose the inspiration I now feel. That inspiration must come from God. I cannot explain it any other way. Don't you believe that, Father?"

"Of course I do. I try, in all that I undertake, to let myself be guided by Providence, but it is difficult to discern God's will, believe me. Sometimes it turns out to be my own will that I am seeking instead of God's. I would suggest that you give this more thought and that you pray over it. I will do the same. One thing I must say however. If the project you speak of does not come into the direct line of work that the Brothers do, then I cannot let even one or two of them work with you."

"Oh, but I have seen the Brothers at work. Everybody is talking about them! Your Sunday School is very much like what I have in mind, only I would take the boys much younger and would keep them a longer time to complete their education."

"I do not want to discourage you by any means. I am going to give you a copy of a memorandum I drew up some time ago to explain the origin and the purpose of our Society. Study it carefully, then come and see me again. Are you willing to do that?"

"Most willing."

Father de La Salle turned toward me.

"In the desk drawer on the left, Brother François, you will find several copies of the memorandum. Will you hand me one of them, please?"

I found the copies and handed one to Father de La Salle who gave it to Clément.

"This will help you understand the work of the Brothers. I will be happy to discuss it with you on another occasion," Father de La Salle said, as the two shook hands. "And thank you for the confidence you have shown in coming here today."

I accompanied Clément to the door and we said good-bye. I have not forgotten Father de La Salle's last words to me that morning.

"It seems strange, Brother François. I wonder who is really behind this project. Is it the bishop of Chartres or the Abbot of Saint-Calais or Father de La Chétardye? Or is it really Providence who has inspired this young man with such noble sentiments?"

Father de La Salle was to see much more of the future Abbot of Saint-Calais in the weeks and months following that first meeting. In fact, in less than a week Clément was back, bubbling with enthusiasm. Father de La Salle told us about the meeting and how the young Abbé had decided to give up his original idea. He now wanted to open a training college for teachers and promised to use the revenue from the Abbey of Saint-Calais to offer twenty scholarships to young men who would come to the college. He had even found a house in the suburb of Saint Antoine for the purpose. Not only did he entreat Father de La Salle once more to give him two Brothers to teach in the training college, but he asked him outright to lend him several thousand livres to make a down payment on the house.

Ever since the unfortunate departure of Nicholas Vuyart and the collapse of the college of Saint Hippolytus, Father de La Salle had been seeking ways and means of establishing another to take its place. At this moment, in fact, he was in possession of the sum of 5,200 livres, which had been given him for this purpose. The unexpected proposal of Clément fell in with his plans, but there were obstacles in the way. In the first place, Father de La Salle, having lost his last lawsuit with the Writing Masters, had received a formal court order forbidding him to open a school or to establish an institution for the training of schoolmasters anywhere in the Paris area until his Society was recognized and approved by the Parliament. This immediately ruled out Clément's idea of acquiring a house in the Saint Antoine suburb. Besides this, Clément himself, only twenty-two years of age, was a minor in the eyes of the law, and therefore incapable of disposing of large sums of money by contract. Hence, despite Clemént's enthusiasm and despite his desire to accomplish something immediately, Father de La Salle felt obliged to restrain him and wait on circumstances.

This, of course, was not to Clément's satisfaction. However, he was not easily discouraged. For months on end he continued to importune our superior by letters and by visits. Then he came to me asking for help. He was curious to learn something about Nicolas Vuyart and the reasons for his failure when he was in charge of the training college. It seemed strange to me that he wanted in some way to repair the harm done to our Society by that unfaithful disciple. I wondered, too, how he had learned that Father de La Salle had money put aside to reestablish the training college.

A whole year went by and still our superior hesitated to come to an agreement. Then Clément, impatient at such a long delay, took the matter into his own hands in the hope of forcing Father de La Salle to do something. He sought the approval of the Cardinal Archbishop of Paris for the project. This was the normal procedure. Evidently, nothing could be done without the Cardinal's approval, but Clément's action caught Father de La Salle by surprise. The Cardinal was favorable, thanks to the intervention of the Bishop of Chartres and the Abbot of Saint-Calais. He set down only one condition. The training college had to be located outside of Paris, where it would not attract the animosity of the Writing Masters or come under the interdiction of the city courts.

With so many important people now interested in reopening the training college, it became more and more evident to Father de La Salle that he might indeed have to reach an agreement of some kind. A very close friend of his, Father Charles de La Grange, pastor of Villiers-le-Bel, a village well outside Paris, offered a place for the college and the Brothers' residence. The idea pleased Father de La Salle all the more since in this parish resided a certain Monsieur Sellier whose four sons had entered our Society and who was planning to become a Brother one day himself. What better example than the Sellier family could there be to motivate other young men to enter the training college and become teachers for the villages of the area?

Unfortunately, the prospect of the college at Villiers-le-Bel did not satisfy Monsieur l'Abbé Clément, who considered that locality too far from Paris. Father de La Salle listened to Clément's objection and continued to pray about his decision.

A more suitable situation came to light some time later. Mademoiselle Poignant, a rich lady residing in Paris, offered to help Father de La Salle open a school at Saint Denis not far from the capital. For some time she had been asking for Brothers to take charge of a charity school which she wished to establish with her own money and endow with funds in her will. Now, finally, Father de La Salle was able to accede to her request. With the added encouragement of the Prior of the Monastery of Saint Denis, the school was opened in 1708. It was sufficiently far from Paris to escape the notice of the Writing Masters but the distance was really not too inconvenient. Saint Denis, in fact, could also be the ideal place for the training college Clément was trying to set up. Father de La Salle continued to ponder the matter.

I happened to be with Father de La Salle at Saint Denis some months later when, by sheer coincidence, we met Monsieur Rogier, who had become a close friend and legal advisor of our superior. To our great surprise, he was in the company of the young cleric Monsieur Clément.

"We have very good news for you, Monsieur de La Salle," Rogier said, after shaking hands with us. "Mademoiselle Poignant's sister has a house here in Saint-Denis that is up for sale. It would be ideal for the training college we are dreaming about. Monsieur Clément and I have taken an option on it with her lawyer and could settle the deal very quickly if you were willing to help us."

"I didn't know you were backing this project, Monsieur Rogier," Father de La Salle said, "or that you even knew Monsieur Clément."

"You are really too discreet, Father. You keep yourself hidden away and don't realize all that is happening around you. Not only do I know Monsieur Clément very well but I am also aware of the considerable success he has had in getting support for, what shall I say, our common project? His father is very influential at Court. He is the King's surgeon, you must remember."

"I should have spoken to you about my father," the young cleric explained. "Our family is to receive titles of nobility very soon. His Majesty has been most gracious. I have also been promised a rich Abbey, as I told you before. A few months ago I had the good fortune of being introduced to Monsieur Rogier, who is your friend and has your entire confidence. That is why I have chosen him to act in my name, since I am still too young to sign legal documents."

"I shall be happy to do anything I can for you both," Rogier said. "Our meeting here today seems very providential. Would you be willing to advance the down payment for the house, Father de La Salle? I can assure you that it is a safe procedure, as you know Mademoiselle Poignant and her sister very well. She is asking 5200 livres for the first year. The price of the house is 13,000. My young friend here will complete the payments in due time and will reimburse you for the down payment as soon as he receives the income from Saint-Calais, which could well be within a few months. I will stand guarantee for you both and will gladly lend my name for the transactions. Monsieur Clément will be the real owner of the house. A wise measure, because it will protect you from any interference on the part of the legal authorities. But we must act quickly, Father de La Salle, or we may lose this excellent opportunity."

"Things have already happened much quicker than I had anticipated," Father de La Salle said. Then he added, "I shall need a few more days to think and to pray about it. Could we meet here this coming Monday? I will give you my answer then."

Within a few days Father de La Salle made a decision in favor of Monsieur Clément. The arrangement concluded by Monsieur Rogier had many favorable aspects, no doubt. Not the least of these was the important fact that our superior could remain anonymous in the transactions and thus, hopefully, avoid the opposition and persecution that his other establishments had faced. The only drawback, it seemed, was the fact that Monsieur Clément was still a minor, but was this not offset by the fact that Monsieur Rogier, who was our superior's trusted friend, had signed the papers in his own name? Rogier had also obtained a written statement from Clément saying that Monsieur de La Salle had advanced the down payment of 5200 livres for the purchase of the house. In the same document, Monsieur l'Abbé Clément promised to reimburse our superior for that same amount. Brother Thomas had also taken part in the negotiations. It was he who made the final arrangements, tended to the adjustments needed in the building and selected the twenty students who were to be trained as teachers.

The college was finally opened late that year, 1709. The event caused great satisfaction in the little circle connected with this foundation. The Cardinal expressed his pleasure to Father de La Salle, thus clearly signifying that he recognized the importance of the Brothers' work, despite the incidents that had occurred in Paris. Madame de Maintenon, the Queen, interested herself in the training college and obtained from the King an exemption for the Brothers from the duty of lodging wounded soldiers in their home. This was a significant concession from a recent royal ordinance since there were thousands of wounded soldiers flocking into Paris every day, bringing reports of disaster on the war front.

The Abbot of the Basilica and the parish priest of Saint Denis were both delighted with the training college. The student teachers assisted them at church services just as they would be called on to do later as teachers in country villages. Monsieur Clément, who esteemed himself the real founder of the college, and paid frequent visits there, was more than satisfied, he was jubilant. Everything seemed to indicate a bright future for this work, which Father de La Salle took so much to heart and which was really his.

The college had hardly opened its doors when, in January, a cold spell like none ever before witnessed set in, paralyzing the whole country. Temperatures dropped far below freezing. The Seine river became solid ice all the way to the sea. Conditions of the utmost severity lasted for several weeks. When the cold let up at last, it became evident that irreparable damage had been done and thousands of families had been ruined. With the already apparent shortage of wheat due to the war, and the increasing number of wounded soldiers and jobless vagabonds, the entire country was threatened with disaster. Nothing now could save us from another appalling famine. Groups of men, women, and children, numbering as many as five hundred, were roaming about in search of food, threatening to burn and pillage everything. A second cold wave, even worse and longer than the first, strewed the countryside with frozen corpses, and left little or no hope for any kind of harvest whatsoever.

Brother Thomas was often reduced to the extremity of begging for alms in the street to keep our community alive. One Sunday he was particularly fortunate, thanks to a beautiful sermon we heard on the subject of almsgiving delivered by a priest named Massillon. We had heard that this young priest was famous for sermons he had delivered at Versailles in the presence of the King and in many churches and cathedrals throughout the country. He was now the director of the seminary of the Oratorian Fathers in Paris and a friend of Father de La Chétardye, who had invited him to preach that Sunday at Saint Sulpice.

"Was there ever such misery?" he exclaimed, "Misery in our streets and in public places; misery hidden behind closed doors, hidden through shame and fear of humiliation? Were there ever so many ruined families, so many citizens, respectable yesterday, and today grovelling in the dust with the worst outcasts of society? Where have we ever seen such a specter of starvation and death lurking in our cities and villages and stalking the countryside?"

The eloquence of his words especially when he spoke of the merit of almsgiving inspired many wealthy parishioners to come to the aid of the poor and the hungry in the parish. We were among those who benefited by these acts of generosity, but that source dwindled little by little and then disappeared altogether.

If our situation in Paris seemed almost hopeless, that of the ten Brothers and twenty novices in Rouen was desperate. Father de La Salle was in a terrible dilemma. Could he bring them all to Paris where we were already on the verge of starvation? He finally decided to bring only the novices, but this more than doubled the number of those already living in our home on La Barouillère Street. The house was reasonably spacious for those of us teaching in Paris but far too small to accommodate the new arrivals. They had to sleep on straw mats stretched out on the floor wherever there was some space available. Yet as poor as this house of Providence was, it was open to anyone who wished to enter. Father de La Salle's charity did not shut the door to anyone who showed good will and who was not evidently driven to enter by starvation. Several of the Brothers, however, took it amiss that he should share with newcomers the bread which was often insufficient for ourselves.

One of the most outspoken was Brother Siméon Pajot. He had entered our Society at Vaugirard. I thought that the poverty experienced during his novitiate there would have prepared him to accept our present situation, but he had been spoiled at the Grand'Maison where he had been in charge of the garden and could always find something extra to satisfy his hunger. I knew too, that he had taken sides openly against Brother Michael in the conflict that had almost disrupted our Society, and that now he sided with Father de La Chétardye.

One Sunday afternoon during this difficult period, we had all gathered at our home on La Barouillère Street and were waiting for Father de La Salle to return. He had just gone out with a priest friend of ours, Father Deschamps from Rouen, who had given us a short talk on the terrible situation in his native city. The conversation in the room seemed more animated than usual. Perhaps it was because we were all nervous and hungry and did not know what fate awaited us from day to day. I heard the voice of Brother Siméon dominating the others. He was standing near the middle of the room with his back to the door.

"Why does Deschamps come preaching to us?" Brother Siméon was saying. "He has everything he needs. I'd gladly go to live with him till this famine is over. That is, if I thought we could get along together. But, regardless of what he says, we can't keep on taking in everyone that comes to our door. Enough is enough. Why don't you do something about it, Brother Thomas? Isn't that part of your job?"

"Father de La Salle is the one who accepts or rejects those asking to enter our community," Brother Thomas answered. "You know that, Siméon. I for one have absolute faith in his judgment. What about you? Do you trust him?"

While Brother Thomas and Brother Siméon were discussing, Father de La Salle had entered the room and stepped forward.

"Brother Siméon," he said very calmly, "I see that you, and perhaps some of the other Brothers, are worrying about our increasing numbers. Don't you think that it is just as simple for the Lord to care for thirty or fifty or a hundred as for ten or twelve? For us to determine a certain number would be putting a limit to his liberality. But I do see your point. If you or Brother Barthélemy or any of the Brothers can show me that one or other of these young men asking to enter our Society is here only to avoid starvation, then I will be the first to examine his motives and send him away. He will at least have had the time to make a good retreat while staying with us and that could be useful for his salvation."

Then Father de La Salle turned and walked to the window. With his back to us, he said quietly but with a steady voice, "If some of you prefer to leave the community, I will not try to prevent you, if in your hearts you feel that you cannot live in these conditions any longer. You will be welcome to come back after this crisis is over."

We were deeply moved by his words. There was a reverent silence in the room. Several minutes passed. Then Father de La Salle added in a low, tired voice,

"Does anyone else want to say something?"

No one spoke up. A strange calm seemed to have come over the assembly as Father de La Salle turned and addressed all of us, now with more firmness.

"I want you to know that the Brothers in Rouen, in Reims and in Chartres are in the same situation as we are. They too are a prey to hunger, to cold and to every privation, but Providence is taking care of them as it is taking care of us. As for Saint Denis, I have closed the training college and the charity school there for the time being. God willing, they will open again soon. The four Brothers will remain here with us. I do not know yet what will happen to the schools here in the parish of Saint Sulpice. Father de La Chétardye is undecided.

The words of our superior were encouraging, but we had by no means seen the end of our tribulations.

The extreme poverty of the house and the overcrowded living conditions occasioned the outbreak of what we thought was a contagious disease. Six Brothers came down with scurvy. Thousands of people had already died of the dreaded disease in Paris and it would surely have wrought havoc in our community as well, if Father de La Salle had not at once separated the sick Brothers from the others and had not taken care of them himself. Not being able to pay for the expensive treatment needed to cure them, he went to see Doctor Helvetius, the physician who had saved his own life on one occasion more than fifteen years before. Ever since that time, Dr. Helvetius had remained his good and trusted friend and had often helped the Brothers in time of illness without charging any fees. He now came to the rescue once more by convincing another distinguished doctor in Paris, who had the reputation for curing scurvy, to administer his treatment to the sick Brothers.

Within a few weeks, all of the six Brothers were showing signs of recovery. I could not help but think that their cure was just as much due to Father de La Salle's unselfish care as it was to the doctor's intervention. Our superior had been admirable in caring for the sick Brothers, surely knowing all the while that he might contract the illness himself and that in his case it might well be fatal.

Month after month passed and gradually our situation improved. Several of the young men who had arrived within the year and whose motives for entering our Society may not have been as sincere as Father de La Salle had imagined, left the community of their own accord and returned to their homes. No one had been sent away.

Father de La Salle was finally able to reopen the training college and the charity school at Saint Denis. The success of these two institutions brought him an increase of popularity but it also increased the jealousy of those who wanted to see him replaced as superior of the Brothers. He had withdrawn from Saint Roch's parish and had taken up residence once more with us on La Barouillère Street during the terrible famine.

17

Oɴᴇ ᴘᴀʀᴛɪᴄᴜʟᴀʀ ᴀғᴛᴇʀɴᴏᴏɴ, at the school on Princess Street, Brother Paul Narra came to me nervous and excited. He had turned out to be a very talented young Brother for whom I had great esteem. He taught writing and religion and arithmetic during the ordinary school day and took several gifted students for art classes after school. What could be bothering him today? It was most unusual to see him in such a state.

"Brother François, you should go over to the weaving shop," he said, almost out of breath. "Something has happened. There has been an accident. It's Maurice. He's been hurt."

At the mention of Maurice, I was startled. In all the years I had seen him at work in the weaving shop, there had never been a serious accident. I hurried through the courtyard and reached the shop in less than a minute. Inside, four or five boys were tossing bolts of cloth frantically right and left. There was a huge pile on the floor and it took me only a moment to realize that Maurice was buried underneath. Brother Siméon, who was in charge of the shop, was nowhere to be seen.

I helped the lads as best I could and uncovered the arms and then the head of Maurice. He was staring at me in surprise and fear. I recalled the time I had been in the same fix, only drowned in a pile of light wool, nothing like the weight pressing down on him now.

"What on earth, Maurice! How did this happen? Are you hurt?"

"I don't think so, but please get me out of here. The shelves collapsed, but I don't see how they could have broken. It's next to impossible!" As he brushed himself off, he added, now with a twinkle in his eye, "You're a great one to come to my rescue, François. It's two to one now." He grabbed my hand. "Thanks."

Maurice had no serious injuries, just a few bruises and a bit of shock. I closed the shop, sent the boys home and helped Maurice to his room on the second floor above the classrooms.

We sat down on his couch together. He put his arms around my shoulders and hugged me.

"Thank you, François," he said again.

"Don't thank me, Maurice. I owe this to you and much more."

"You know, François, those shelves couldn't have collapsed of themselves. Someone has been tampering with things in the shop. I am sure of it."

"What do you mean? It's impossible. The boys would never do a thing like that. Who? Who?"

"Let me tell you what I think. You remember when the Brothers—you were one of them—took over the school from Monsieur l'Abbé Compagnon? Rafrond was the boss in the weaving shop. Well, Rafrond especially didn't like it, and both he and Compagnon caused you a lot of trouble, didn't they? I think something like that is happening now. Father de La Chétardye doesn't like Father de La Salle. He never did. I think that if he could take over this school, leaving your superior out of the picture, he would be the happiest man in the world. He has approached me, indirectly of course, to find out just where I stand. I have made it clear that I will stand for you and for Father de La Salle at any cost. I should have become a Brother, François, years ago. Is it too late?"

"Of course not. You would be more than welcome in our Society. But what you say intrigues me. How does it fit in?"

"Brother Siméon, too, has tried to find out how I feel. He is very comfortable with Father de La Chétardye, I think you know that. Since I made my position very clear, there have been things happening in the shop that I don't understand. Little things at first: the lads, it seems are not working hard enough, according to the pastor. But it never fails, something goes wrong with the looms. It's never happened before. We're not making enough profit, he says. You know, François, that Father de La Salle and you yourself never looked for profit. You were always interested in teaching the lads the trade. Am I right? And now this. There's no reason in the world why those shelves should have collapsed. I wouldn't be in the least surprised if tomorrow Brother Siméon asked me to resign. He would say that Father de La Chétardye doesn't want me here any more."

"Don't worry, Maurice. You rest. I'll talk to Brother Theodore and Brother Paul and see what they have to say."

"Brother Siméon has forbidden Brother Paul to come into the shop any more. Do you know that? Paul's a wonderful person. For years he's helped me with designs. All the artistic work is his. It comes to him naturally. He feels hurt, I think, because he can't come any more. He just might do what you tried to do once, remember?"

Paul Narra had been one of the little tots staring up at me that day, not knowing what to do. I had chased him from the classroom with the others, not remembering that he had no home to go to. I could still see him, frightened and stumbling up the stairs, to find safety in Maurice's arms.

"I'm going to talk to him right now, Maurice. I'll get to the bottom of this as soon as possible. Will you be all right?"

"Sure. Don't worry. If it had been that old rascal Potier, I might not be alive to laugh about it. You too ought to take care, François. God bless you."

I gave him a hug, then headed down the stairs in search of Brother Paul. I found that he had replaced Brother Theodore in the yard and was watching the boys at play.

"Why don't you join in the game?" I said, laughing.

"Can you see me playing leapfrog in this robe, François? You have to be joking. I used to, though. Do you remember?"

"I remember a lot of things, Paul. I was just talking to Maurice about my first years here when you were in my class."

"Is he going to be all right? I can't understand how those shelves collapsed like that."

"He was more frightened than hurt. It's strange. You just quoted his exact words. He also told me that you are not allowed to go to the shop any more. Is that so?"

"Yes, it happened about three weeks ago. I'm a bit sad, but then I have my painting, so it's all right."

"What happened three weeks ago, Brother Paul? I need to know."

"Well, I was returning from an errand that afternoon and I had some new designs I wanted to give Maurice. I thought I might find him in the shop on the corner. I almost never go to that little store. But Maurice was not there. I found it odd that the door was open, so I went in to look for him in the back room. Do you know, Brother François, that there is a kind of secret passage from there to the weaving shop in our courtyard?"

"Yes, Maurice showed it to me once. I had gone into the store from the street, trying to escape from the jeering and rowdiness of Marcel Potier."

"How curious. Whom do you think I met coming from that passageway? Brother Siméon and Marcel Potier. I don't know what they were doing there, but I do know that Brother Siméon was very angry at finding me there. He said that I was never to enter that store again, nor even the weaving shop; that it was his domain; that from then on he would take care of the things I had been doing for Maurice; that all this was not his idea, but that Father de La Chétardye didn't want me around any more. Can you believe it?"

"That agrees with what Maurice told me. It seems that the pastor doesn't want him either, now that Brother Siméon has mastered the trade. But what does it all mean? It is no secret that Father de La Chétardye has tried several times to have Father de La Salle replaced as our superior. What could he be up to now? Do you have any idea, Brother Paul?"

"I think I do. I should have told you this a long time ago, but I really thought that nothing would come of it and I didn't want to hurt Brother Siméon. He came to me to say that Father de La Chétardye was looking for a place near here where he could lodge the Brothers working in the parish, make their life more comfortable, and give them a better salary.

"I thought at first that through the goodness of his heart— and the pastor does love us a great deal—that this would alleviate the situation at La Barouillère Street. But now I know that something is afoot."

Brother Paul paused to get my reaction, but I kept quiet and continued to listen. He went on.

"Brother Siméon, it seems, would be the superior in the new residence. He would receive the salaries of all the Brothers working in the parish schools. None of it could any longer be used to support the novitiate or the house on La Barouillère Street. Brother Siméon, in fact, would be the new superior of our Society. Father de La Salle would have to retire."

Brother Paul was embarrassed he had not told me all this before. After a moment, he continued.

"Of course, when I realized what this meant, I refused to have any part in it. That is certainly why I have been ostracized from the weaving shop. Father de La Chétardye and Brother Siméon both thought that because I have been here since I was a student myself, I would go along with their plan. They didn't think I would say anything about it. In fact, they asked me not to. I'm sorry not to have spoken sooner, Brother François. I hope it's not too late to stop them."

"Do you know if any other Brothers have accepted to break away from our community?"

"Only Brother Alexis, who is teaching at our school on St. Placid Street, but I don't think he will stay with us very long anyway. He is unhappy."

"Thank you, Brother Paul. This weekend I'll bring the whole thing out into the open."

We embraced. I could sense the nervousness and embarrassment in him. He was trembling, but I knew that I could count on him. I didn't have the courage at that moment to confront Brother Siméon. I would do that in front of all the Brothers and Father de La Salle at our next assembly.

The following Sunday was a memorable day in the history of our Society. Father de La Salle wanted to celebrate the Eucharist with us in thanksgiving for all the favors we had received during the terrible year of famine that was drawing to a close. All the schools were now reopened, the training college was functioning wondrously, and news from the Brothers in Reims, Rouen, and Chartres was encouraging.

Father de La Salle had spoken movingly. There could be no question as to who was guiding and protecting our Society: Divine Providence was at the helm. We had nothing to fear. It was God's work. He would see it through. As was his custom, our superior asked the Brother in charge of each school to express his opinion. Brother Clément Gatelet spoke well of his work with Brother Marc Morel at the school on Du Bac Street. Brother Ponce did not seem quite as sure of himself when he spoke about the school on St. Placid Street, but he did not criticize his helper, Brother Alexis Jourdain.

When my turn came to speak, I was overcome by emotion. How could I bring up the subject that had been haunting me now for several days? How would Brother Théodore Sellier, to whom I had not even spoken about the impending confrontation, feel in this situation, and how would Brother Paul react, having had time to think about it all? But, most of all, what would Brother Siméon do?

"Father de La Salle," I said, "there is something happening at the weaving shop that I can't quite explain. Father de La Chétardye and Marcel Potier have been seen there recently, and Maurice barely escaped a serious injury several days ago when the shelves collapsed on him. Brother Paul is not allowed to work there any more after devoting twenty years of his life to that work. You will remember that he was there as a boy when we first came to Paris."

"Of course I remember. I put Brother Siméon in charge of the weaving shop. Will you tell us what has happened, Brother Siméon?"

I had been watching Brother Siméon as the conversation gradually built up to this point. He was fidgety. Now he looked over at me, somewhat bewildered.

"Father," he said, "the lads are not working seriously enough. There is always trouble with the looms. We are not making the profit we should. Father de La Chétardye is dissatisfied. He has asked me to take over the entire direction of the shop. He doesn't want Maurice or Brother Paul there any longer."

"Brother Siméon," Father de La Salle said, "when we accepted to take over the school on Princess Street years ago it was understood that we would have the direction of the weaving shop as well. Is that not so? It was never to be considered a business operation. If some of our students learned the trade and were able to earn a little money, it was to benefit their families, not us."

"Father de La Chétardye wants to change that," Brother Siméon said. "I can't contradict him."

"Excuse me, Father de La Salle," I interrupted. "May I ask Brother Siméon a question?"

"Of course, what is it?"

"It appears that the pastor wants many other things to be different as well, Brother Siméon. Isn't he asking you to do something more than taking over the weaving shop? Something, for example, like founding a little community of your own, under his direction?"

My question caused a stir among the Brothers. It was easy to see that most of them were totally unaware of the conspiracy that had been taking shape in our midst. Father de La Salle showed no particular signs of disturbance. His attention remained fixed on Brother Siméon whose reaction everyone awaited. My inquiry had caused him to stiffen. His face reddened and he stared at me with blazing eyes as he answered.

"Yes, he is asking for something more than the weaving shop, François. Father de La Chétardye wants a community of Brothers in his parish who will listen to reason, who will follow his direction, who will take no risks of starving to death or losing their health for a foolish ideal. I believe he is right. It is time that we go along with him instead of fighting him. He will give those of us who teach in the parish a new residence, a better salary, and less strenuous regulations."

The Brothers in the assembly were bewildered. Everyone began asking questions.

"And who is to be the director of this new community?" Brother Thomas asked.

"The pastor has asked me to take on that responsibility. I have accepted. Naturally he will have the last word."

Brother Siméon's voice trembled as he made that bold statement and became aware of the increasing opposition in the room.

"And the members of the new community?" Brother Thomas continued.

"Any of you who have courage enough to be honest."

"What do you mean to be honest? You have not been honest with us, nor with Father de La Salle. You have been plotting behind his back."

"Am I not speaking openly now? Brother Alexis has already given me his word and there are others." He hesitated. "Speak out. Why don't you speak out?" he shouted angrily.

"I have changed my mind," Brother Alexis said. "I am leaving the Society. The Writing Masters Guild has accepted me. I'm tired of working this hard, of living in these conditions, not knowing where the next meal is going to come from, of sharing the money I earn with all these newcomers."

Before anyone could question him or stop him, he had turned and left the room.

"You would do well to follow him, Siméon," Brother Antoine said, pointing to the door. "Are you trying to start a rebellion against Father de La Salle?"

"This is not a rebellion. It is just plain common sense."

"Then let your common sense take you to the street, Siméon, and your new community with you. We'll hear nothing more of it."

"We'll not listen to Father de La Chétardye," someone else said. "He is not our superior. Father de La Salle is our only superior and we'll have no other. No one wants you for superior, Siméon."

"Please be calm, Brothers." Father de La Salle's voice was unperturbed. "Perhaps we all need a little time to examine the things we've heard before making any rash decisions. I'll talk to Brother Siméon and to anyone else who cares to express his views, but do let us avoid any more public demonstrations."

Father de La Salle was the first to leave the room. A silence as total as it was ominous came over the assembly. One by one, the Brothers began to leave. I waited purposely till the last. No one had said a word. Looking back from the doorway, I saw Brother Siméon, still standing in the middle of the room, alone.

No one was surprised, the following morning, to see Brother Siméon's place in the chapel deserted. His room, too, was empty. I half expected him to show up at school that day or soon afterward, in the company of Father de La Chétardye, but no. We never saw anything of him again.

More surprising still, Father de La Chétardye himself left us completely undisturbed for the next several months. Had he finally decided that he was fighting a losing battle? There were no more strange accidents in the weaving shop, which now came under the skillful direction of Brother Paul Narra.

18

FATHER DE LA SALLE used this peaceful time to finish several books he had been working on. One important book was the "Rules and Regulations," a book which contained our daily routine, the hours of rising and retiring, the schedule of prayer, of meals, and of certain other practices we had agreed to observe to maintain order and discipline in our community life. The "Conduct of Schools" was a book that contained general guidelines for running a school and ideas on methodology to help teach more effectively. It was the result of years of experience in the schools and of community discussions in which we shared ideas and ideals freely with Father de La Salle. The "Duties of a Christian" was a kind of catechism, containing instructions in faith and morality, the sacraments, and prayer. Father de La salle used a simple style in this book to make it very easy to read. In fact, we used it as a reading book in many of our classes.

The "Rules of Decorum and Christian Civility" was one of my favorite books. We used it to teach politeness and good manners. The children in our classes were taught that politeness had to be inspired by Christian charity to be authentic. At the same time, they learned to read the text and to copy passages from the book to improve their handwriting. Father de La Salle wrote the "Explanation of the Method of Mental Prayer" to help the young men coming to the novitiate to pray. It was a kind of spiritual workbook and so practical that all of us used it to help in our own personal prayer, by meditating on the lives of the saints or by reflecting on passages from the Gospel.

With the novitiate now flourishing in Paris, Father de La Salle was able to answer requests for Brothers in Versailles, Moulins, and Boulogne, as well as in several cities in the South, Marseilles, Avignon, Mende, Alais, and Grenoble. The school in the papal territory of Avignon was of particular interest because it brought us into closer relationship with the Holy See, and Father de La Salle was seeking both papal and legal approbation for his young Society. These foundations were financed by the bishops of the area or by small groups of zealous men and women who formed charitable societies for this purpose.

In 1711, while our superior was away visiting these new schools, an unexpected turn of events in Paris showed us that his enemies had profited by his absence to prepare yet another plot against him. We came to learn of this almost by accident.

Brother Antoine, Brother Thomas and I had gone to the Basilica of Saint Denis on a special pilgrimage. As the ceremonies were finishing and we were leaving, I saw Monsieur Clément and pointed him out to Brother Thomas.

"Look at that wig," I said. "He's acting like the King himself."

"He has a right to," Brother Thomas replied. "You know he and his father belong to the nobility now. They are both rich. Clément is the Abbot of Saint-Calais."

"Well then he should have repaid Father de La Salle's loan to him for the training college," Brother Antoine remarked.

"That's all come to nothing," Brother Thomas said. "Clément's no longer interested in the college. He's given up on it. I think his fervor got dampened by his new wealth and prestige."

"Well, what about the loan?" echoed Brother Antoine.

"That's off, too."

"What do you mean?" I insisted.

"I haven't seen any of that loan money," Brother Thomas said. "It was 5,200 livres, if my memory serves me, but I'm afraid Father de La Salle has been robbed by nobility!"

"But Clément gave him or Rogier a receipt for that loan. Rogier was there at the time," I said, recalling the incident. "I intend to wait right here until Clément leaves the crowd. I want to ask him about that loan."

A few minutes later, Monsieur Clément came out of the basilica in the company of several other clergymen. My coarse black robe and mantle with flowing sleeves contrasted with their rich attire, but I was neither embarrassed nor intimidated.

"Good morning, Monsieur l'Abbé," I said when Clément was near me. "I am Brother François. I was with Father de La Salle when you made the agreement with him about the training college here. Perhaps you remember? The Brothers have not seen you for some time now. Would you like to come to the house together with your friends?"

"I'm afraid I have no time for that any more. I have many more important things to think about now that I am the Abbot of Saint-Calais. This college does not interest me in the least. In fact, I intend to sell the property soon. The matter is in the hands of my lawyers.

"But what about the money that Father de La Salle lent you to purchase it? You must return it to him. We are in dire need of it."

"You are misinformed, Brother. That is out of the question. It was Monsieur Rogier who negotiated with him. Speak to him. Furthermore, you may inform the Brothers in my name that they will have to leave the training college very soon. They will be notified by my lawyer. I am leaving the city for several months. Au revoir, Brother François."

I hurried into the house to break this sorry news only to learn that the Brothers had been fearing the worst ever since Father de La Salle had left. We decided at once to send him an urgent message. The situation was extremely serious and his presence in Paris was indispensable.

Several weeks went by before Father de La Salle returned. He told us of the new foundations in the South and how bright the future of the Society looked there. It was difficult for us to burden him anew with the dangers that threatened our Society in Paris.

One afternoon, shortly after his return, I was startled by the incessant clanging of the bell in the courtyard. I went running to open the door. A gentleman whom I had never seen before stood there pulling angrily at the bell cord. His carriage and coachman were waiting in the street.

"Good afternoon, Monsieur," I said. "Welcome to the Brothers' house. Won't you come in?"

"I need no welcome, Monsieur. My business will take little time. Is Monsieur de La Salle here? I have come to unmask his duplicity."

The King's surgeon, Julien Clément, accuses De La Salle of extorting money from his son to found a training college for teachers.

"His duplicity!" I controlled my anger and said, "He is here. I'll go for him. May I ask who is calling?"

"Julien Clément, surgeon to his Royal Majesty Louis XIV and father of Monsieur l'Abbé Jean-Charles Clément, whom your superior has defrauded of a small fortune."

"Defrauded!" I gasped.

"I'll speak with Monsieur de La Salle," he said defiantly.

Stunned, I turned away to call Father de La Salle, but he too had heard the clamor of the bell and was coming toward us.

"Will you come in, Monsieur?" he asked calmly.

"There is no need. You are speaking with Monsieur Julien Clément, surgeon to his Royal Majesty Louis XIV and father of Monsieur Jean-Charles Clément, Abbé de Saint-Calais," he repeated with dignity. "I have come here to warn you, Monsieur de La Salle, that if you do not vacate the training college at Saint Denis and return the money you tricked my son into investing in that enterprise, I'll take you to court. You took advantage of a minor. I'll ruin you and all your establishments."

"There was no trickery, Monsieur. You are distorting the facts. If your son invested some money in the training college, he did so of his own free will. Furthermore, I personally lent him 5,200 livres to make a down payment on the house. He kept insisting on borrowing it. He signed a receipt. Brother François here was a witness."

"A falsification! You tricked him into signing it! But I am not interested in that. I am here to retrieve the money that he himself invested. I swear to God I'll get that money back! My son could not accept such a loss; he was too young, too immature as well, I might add. His honor and mine are at stake."

"Please stop insulting me, Monsieur Clément. I loaned money to your son in good faith and for a good cause. Your son was to return it to the Brothers in due time. I insist that he do so. Bring your son here. He cannot deny the truth."

"My son has left Paris for an indefinite period. He cannot stand the humiliation that this affair has brought upon him."

"Neither can I nor the Brothers stand the insults you are heaping upon us."

"You are an impostor, a hypocrite. I swear that I shall take every means in my power to avenge my son. Beware, Monsieur de La Salle. You are walking on dangerous ground. I will see you in court and I will have you condemned."

The whole affair was outrageous, unjust, dishonest, but it had been carefully and cleverly prepared. We felt, nevertheless, that Father de La Salle's innocence would be proved and his honor restored.

He took every precaution to prepare his defense, drawing up a detailed account of the entire matter, providing papers and letters proving the validity of his position. He was even willing to abandon his right to the property if need be, in order to settle out of court and to save the training school.

He put all these proofs into the hands of lawyers, friends of long standing, asking them to intervene in his favor. Then he disappeared.

But all Father de La Salle's efforts were to no avail. The evidence he had gathered was presented in court by his lawyers in a distorted way. They had been won over by his opponents. His ecclesiastical superiors had also taken sides with Clément. His friends had betrayed him.

The climax of it all came when Monsieur Rogier, who had once been our Superior's intimate friend and adviser and who was deeply implicated in the affair himself, came in person to bring us the first pronouncement of the court and then left without out a word of explanation. According to the document, the court had annulled Clément's debt to us of 5,200 livres, confiscated the building and ordered our superior to reimburse all moneys invested by Clément for the upkeep of the training college. That was an additional 2,300 livres. The court had judged this money to have been extorted from a minor. Father de La Salle was ordered to appear at the next hearing of the court or face imprisonment.

It was unbelievable, but what could we do? Brother Barthélemy and I contacted Father de La Salle in his place of retreat and took the document to him. We watched in sadness, hoping that our presence might alleviate the pain the document would inflict.

He read it slowly, several times. Then he rose and walked silently toward the window, where he stood with his back to us. He seemed crushed and disillusioned. What made the situation even worse, as I learned only later, was that Father de La Salle thought at that moment that some of his own Brothers had also turned against him. The treachery of Nicholas Vuyart was still on his mind.

Night was falling, the tiled roofs dissolving in the gray mist slowly enveloping the towers of the cathedral. When he turned, Father de La Salle's features seemed tired and strained. He murmured to himself:

"Monsieur Rogier and my own Brothers . . . " but he said no more.

Sitting down again, he lowered his head into his hands and remained motionless for a long while.

"May I send up something for supper, Father?" I said. "It's too hard on you, so much fasting."

"No. Thank you, Brother François. I would prefer to be alone now. I will return to the Brothers' house later tonight."

We left him and returned heavy-hearted through the fog and cold to La Barouillère Street. We imagined that Father de La Salle would spend the night in prayer as was his custom in times of crisis.

His situation was indeed extremely critical. His every move was judged suspicious; persecution beset him on all sides; he no longer had any friends; he was even in danger of being thrown into prison. During the night he was to come to one of the most crucial decisions of his life.

I had gone to my room, lit the candle in front of the image of Our Lady and stretched out fully dressed on my couch. There was no way I could find sleep. Well after the last curfew had sounded midnight and the noises of the city had subsided, I became suddenly aware that someone was in the hallway outside my door. I sat up quickly. Had the candlelight at that late hour attracted someone's attention? There was a faint tapping on the door.

"What is it?" I whispered. "Who's there?"

"Brother Barthélemy," came the answer

I pushed the door open about halfway. "Brother Barthélemy, what's the matter?"

"It's Father de La Salle," he said, his voice trembling. "He wants to see you, Brother François. Go there quickly. Try to stop him from leaving us."

"Leaving?"

"Yes, he'll tell you. Go now."

I found the door of Father de La Salle's room open. I did not know when he had returned. He beckoned me to come in.

"Did Brother Barthélemy tell you?" he asked quietly.

"Not really, Father. He said something about your leaving. I don't understand."

"Brother François, I am thoroughly convinced that I am of no use here any longer. On the contrary, I have become a very serious obstacle to the work, to God's work."

"This hurricane won't do any more harm than the others. See how the Brothers are united behind you, Father."

"Thank them for me. God bless them all. I want you to understand well what I say, Brother François. I made a very serious mistake in dealing with the young Abbé Clément. He was not yet twenty-five. The Court is right. I should have known better. I should not have loaned him the money in the first place. It's entirely my fault, just as Nicolas Vuyart's leaving was my fault. I should never have exposed him to the danger of leaving the Society by allowing the pastor to put that money in his name. These errors and many others are convincing signs to me that I am not capable of governing the Society any longer. I have no choice but to leave Paris."

"Leave!"

"Yes, and hopefully save our Society. God wants it to continue. I am sure of that."

"As he willed that you remain at its head."

"In the beginning, yes! Now, I don't know. Remember Monsieur Nyel? God rest his soul! He knew how to disappear when he had given his full measure."

"You have no obligation to follow the example of Monsieur Nyel."

"Every difficulty we've encountered has invariably involved me personally."

"It would have been the same with anyone else."

"I'm less sure of that. Of all the obstacles I have had to overcome, the most difficult is to see clearly within myself. Have I become so comfortably installed in authority that it is now impossible to accept anybody else's way of thinking?"

"Why do you attach so much importance to this unfortunate Clément business."

"Because it may be the sign that I have departed from the ways of Providence. And when one is lost, who knows how long and hard it is to find the way again? At least, while I'm gone, trouble here will disappear."

"The Brothers won't understand. They'll accuse you of deserting."

"May all the accusations counterbalance the exaggerated amount of good that has been attributed to me. I have confided the government of the Society to Brother Barthélemy. Eventually, the Brothers must elect him or another Brother as superior. He will govern the Society with love, I am sure of it."

Father de La Salle drew me close to him with great affection and traced a cross on my forehead before we parted.

"Keep this confidential until I'm gone. Will you, Brother François?" he said softly.

Only the next morning when the Brothers met for prayer, did I feel the full impact of what had happened.

Father de La Salle's place was empty.

19

THAT THE SUPERIOR of the Brothers should be absent from Paris was nothing unusual. Father de La Salle loved solitude more than anything else. He often disappeared for days or weeks at a time, going to some monastery or other to escape from the world, to pray, or to write. He did this particularly when he had some important decision to make or problem to solve. The more severe the crisis that faced him, the longer he would remain in solitude. He wanted to make very sure that he was doing God's will and not his own. We had become accustomed to his disappearing like this.

For some time already, he had placed many details of the government of the Society in the hands of capable Brothers. He had shown total confidence in Brother Barthélemy as director of the novitiate for the formation of new members. Things had always gone smoothly during his absence. The fact that Father de La Salle made no appearance at court, as the Clément lawsuit unfolded, or that he did not return to our community in Paris, aroused no apprehension at the time. We simply imagined that he would return when the tempest had subsided, as he had always done in the past. But when days began to grow into weeks, and weeks into months, and still no word came from him, we began to feel extremely uneasy.

Our enemies in Paris were the first to take advantage of the situation. The Clément lawsuit came to an end—a disastrous end for Father de La Salle. The fact that he had financial dealings with a minor ruined his reputation in the eyes of many who had previously held him in great esteem. The sentence of the Court went so far as to refuse him the title of superior of the Brothers in Paris, a confirmation of the Cardinal's decision.

I hoped that Father de La Chétardye would not take advantage of the situation to interfere once more in the government of the Society.

More than a year passed and still no word came from Father de La Salle. We wondered if he had taken refuge in some hidden monastery far from Paris. He had often told us that we should try seriously to get on without him. Perhaps he had finally decided to put us to the test. Yet, it was not at all like him to give up in the face of opposition. Perhaps he had gone to visit the new foundations in the South.

Our situation in Paris was becoming more and more critical every day. The absence of Father de La Salle forced us to accept the full authority of Brother Barthélemy, though at first some of the older members of the Society had shown signs of resentment. Brother Barthélemy was kind and understanding but unfortunately not strong enough to resist the pressure of a man like Father de La Chétardye who quickly learned that he could now play the leading role. He got the Cardinal to name Monsieur de Brou as the ecclesiastical superior of the Brothers.

De La Chétardye and de Brou then drew up an entirely new set of rules and regulations for the Society and submitted them to the Cardinal for approval.

Word of this reached Brother Barthélemy, who had the courage and foresight to call a meeting of the principal Brothers in Paris. He spoke to us very frankly about the dangers we were up against and suggested that together we try to locate Father de La Salle and oblige him to return to Paris. He revealed for the first time that our superior had given him a name and address where he could be reached in case of urgent necessity. The name was that of a priest, Richelot, who lived in the village of Alais not far from Avignon, in the South.

Brother Barthélemy's plan was to send a letter to Father de La Salle asking him to return. It was to be more than a request; it would be an order given in the name of the body of the Society to which Father de la Salle had vowed obedience, as we all had done—an order to return immediately and resume his duties as superior. It was to be signed by all of us.

The boldness of this proposition was apparent to everyone, but we believed that the extreme urgency of the situation demanded bold action. I could not help but recall how Nicolas Vuyart had used the same strategy of appealing to the consensus of the principal Brothers to oblige Father de La Salle to accept his election as superior of our community in 1694. If we could locate him, there would be no question about his reaction. He would obey.

Brother Barthélemy chose me to be the messenger. Though deeply pleased to have been chosen, I was frightened by the serious responsibility involved in such a mission.

I set out early the next morning, the last words of Brother Barthélemy still ringing in my ears: "Remember, Brother François, the life of our Society could well be in your hands."

After many long days of travel, mostly by carriage, but occasionally on horseback, I reached Avignon, far to the South in the Rhone valley. The imposing castle of the Popes with its enormous quadrangular towers dominated the ancient city.

Brother Timothée, the superior in the area, was surprised and happy to see me, but the news he had of Father de La Salle was not encouraging. The long journey on foot from Paris a year before had been very difficult on him and had renewed the pain of his rheumatism.

"He left here after resting a few weeks," Brother Timothée said, "intending to visit the community in Marseille and then take a boat to Rome to visit Brother Gabriel Drolin, who has been away from France for more than ten years."

I was saddened at the news of Father de La Salle's suffering and set out at once in the hope of reaching him in Marseille on his return from Rome. Brother Timothée dissuaded me from going to Alais in the high mountain country to the West of the Rhone valley in search of Father Richelot, for two reasons: because of the Camisard rebellion in that area and because he felt sure that Father de La Salle was not there.

From the old port in the heart of Marseille, I made my way to the Brothers' school. Our superior had indeed taken passage on a boat bound for Rome, but at the last minute the bishop had appeared at the port and pleaded with him to stay in the city for some time longer in order to take over another school. Father de La Salle sacrificed his journey to Rome to try to work out details for this new foundation. The project failed, however, when several key Brothers he had asked to take over the school abruptly decided to leave the Society.

This also brought about the ruin of the novitiate Father de La Salle had opened in Marseille several months after his arrival. These sad events had all happened in the spring of 1713, more than a year ago.

One of the priests of the city told me that Father de La Salle had left Marseille after this disappointment, convinced that his presence was causing controversy, there as elsewhere.

"He went to La Sainte Baume during Holy Week last year to make a retreat," the priest said. "That's a rugged mountain area near here. The austerity of the place is frightening. However, there is a monastery in the vicinity where one can stay. Brother François, I can't help but worry about your superior. He is not well. I suppose you know."

"Do you think he might have retired there secretly? We have not had any word from him and don't know where he is."

"The only way to find out is to go there yourself, Brother. It is a rough and dangerous road. I wish you well and may God bless you."

A deep feeling of sorrow flooded over me. I had to find him, as much for myself now as for him. The next day I set out for La Sainte Baume and the monastery of Saint Maximin.

Several hours after leaving Marseille, the road became a steep rocky path winding its way toward a distant summit. I climbed on, higher and higher, amid thorny bushes, huge white boulders, stunted pines bent into strange shapes by the southern winds, and genista bushes in full bloom, their golden flowers and green needles contrasting beautifully with the lavender plants that huddled here and there among the rocks.

I thought of Father de La Salle every minute of the way, praying that no evil had befallen him. When I reached the foot of a tremendous rock cliff overlooking the plains below, I paused to rest. Toward the north, the path led to a shelter in the rock wall, a natural grotto where tradition had it that Mary Magdalen had spent the last years of her life. I half expected to find Father de La Salle kneeling there in the semi darkness.

Pilgrims before me had left burning candles on the altar. I lit one myself and placed it at the foot of the large crucifix that adorned the grotto, thinking all the while that Father de La Salle must surely have said Mass on this very spot. I rested for an hour or so and then began the descent toward the north where the monastery of Saint Maximin was located.

Here I learned that Father de La Salle had spent more than a month with the monks and would have liked to stay on till the end of his days.

"He seemed very undecided as to what he should do," the prior told me. "He had even thought of retiring to some country village where he might exercise his priestly ministry toward the poor and remain entirely unknown. He left without telling us where he was going."

My only hope now was to find Father Richelot, the priest in Alais who was Brother Barthélemy's contact with Father de La Salle. I had been warned by the superior of the monastery not to venture into the area of Alais, because it was the stronghold of the Camisards, who were a kind of militia organized by the Protestants in the South of France. They were members of the Reformed Church. When the King revoked the Edict of Nantes that had protected them for years, they rose in open rebellion. The Camisards became bitter enemies of the King and of the Roman Church. The royal troops had little chance of victory over them in these mountainous regions where hardly any roads existed. In his eagerness to wipe out Catholicism from this Gévaudan region, the Camisard general had ordered every priest and religious to leave the country under pain of being burnt alive. This was the situation in the territory through which I now had to travel in order to carry out my mission.

I could not travel as a Brother so I took up the disguise of a doctor, in the hope of avoiding suspicion. I cannot deny that I was afraid, but, despite my fear, I knew I had to find Father Richelot. The thought of the desperate situation of the Brothers in Paris and of all the suffering Father de La Salle had been through urged me on. I prayed, half through faith, half through fear, as I plodded along.

After a few days, I fell in with a young lawyer from Avignon, named Antoine Latour. His curiosity I found very hard to satisfy, especially after he learned that I belonged to the medical profession. My experience with Helvetius in administering the cure for acute rheumatism helped me, but, under the barrage of questions that now came my way, I felt helpless. Latour wanted to learn remedies for all sorts of ailments. Happily, I managed to direct the conversation into more comfortable channels. For one thing, I cautiously brought up the subject of Camisards.

Latour seemed to be well informed.

"Did you know," he asked, "that Father Chayla, the superior of the missions in this region, was kidnapped and murdered?"

"Yes, I heard about it in Paris. I understand that the King's soldiers were useless."

"Other priests have been burnt alive. Their churches have been leveled to the ground and their schools pillaged."

I allowed Latour to ramble on. My mind was on Father de La Salle, who must have travelled this same way. The thought that something might have happened to him troubled me.

The last day of the journey took us through a very arid region, where we stopped and shared a meager lunch of bread, dried meat, and fruit. When we were about to set out again, I noticed several men coming in our direction. They all wore blouses made of rough white material reaching well below their waists. The peasants in the area sometimes dressed like this, but I had been told that the Camisards had adopted the same garment. When I turned toward Latour, I saw him taking a similar blouse from the bag beside him. A cold fear began to take hold of me.

"Hello, comrades," Latour called out, slipping the blouse over his head as the strangers approached.

"What brings you back so soon, Antoine?" queried one of them. "And who is your companion here?"

"A physician friend of mine from Marseille, Jacques Delanot, and a great talker he is, too. We've had a good trip together."

"All too short," I said, at the same time greeting the others. "Tell me, how far are we from Alais?"

"Only a matter of an hour or so. You'll have no trouble finding the way," Latour said. "I'm going to accompany these gentlemen to Le Vigan."

"Very well. Au revoir. Perhaps we shall meet again." I watched the party move off in a southeasterly direction. I had only one thought in mind, to put as many miles as I could between myself and this band of Camisards.

In Alais, I learned that Father Richelot's home had been pillaged and burned by the Camisards a few months before. He had barely managed to escape with his life. I found him at the bishop's palace in Mende. He instructed me to continue on to Grenoble and suggested I go by way of Les Vans. There was a Brothers' community and school in Les Vans and I needed no encouragement to use that route, though it took me another day. I found the Brothers there discouraged and preoccupied. Their school too had been attacked, but fortunately the King's soldiers had arrived in the city in time to disperse the vandals. The Brothers hoped that would be the last of the uprisings. The Camisard rebellion was now dying out.

But the best news was that Father de La Salle had visited the community before these attacks. "He was worn out," the director of the community told me. "I've never seen him so physically tired and disillusioned. He hardly spoke with us. He rested for two days and then went to visit a friend of his, Monsieur Jauffret, who lives in the country beyond Les Vans. I'll take you there tomorrow, Brother François, but Father de La Salle must certainly have gone on to Grenoble, the only community in the South that he had not visited since he left Paris. It has been months now. I am surprised that no one has heard from him."

We found Monsieur Jauffret at home the following evening. He had been able to protect Father de La Salle for several weeks during the worst of the Camisard rebellion and had indeed accompanied him to Grenoble in late July. I liked Jauffret immediately. He was an artist. The hall and parlor of his home were adorned with his paintings. He had been able to do a portrait of our superior on the sly and, when he showed it to us, we were delighted over the remarkable resemblance.

"I don't think he ever knew about it," Monsieur Jauffret said, quite amused. "Otherwise, he would never have allowed me to do it. But come, Brothers, let me offer you a good glass of wine and we'll talk more about this extraordinary superior of yours."

I learned from Monsieur Jauffret that, while in Grenoble, Father de La Salle replaced one of the Brothers in the classroom for more than a month during the past winter. People were still talking about the saintly priest they had seen walking in the street with his young pupils on the way to the church of Saint Lawrence, where he said Mass for them. The winter was extremely cold and Father de La Salle took ill again with rheumatic fever. He was at the point of death and escaped only because he accepted to undergo once more the terrible treatment that Helvetius had used to cure him in Paris in 1690. After this narrow escape, Father de La Salle accepted an invitation from a close friend, Father Yse de Saléon, to replace him as chaplain in a place of pilgrimage called Our Lady of Parménie, in the mountain country north of Grenoble. He had made it clear that no one except this friend, his confessor, and Monsieur Jauffret was to know of his whereabouts. He had expressed the desire to spend the rest of his days there, entirely unknown.

Thus, thanks to Monsieur Jauffret, I finally discovered exactly where I could find Father de La Salle. This kind gentleman even offered to guide me during the last part of my journey as he was obliged to return to Grenoble the following week.

We traveled up the Rhone valley and very often along the river bank. Here and there, on some high isolated spot, we could see the ruins of old castles with their fortifications, the only reminder of the ancient feudal system that had once ruled this part of France.

At Valence, we broke away from the Rhone valley and followed another river, the Isère, which was to lead us to the old Roman town of Tullins. Here Monsieur Jauffret pointed out the way to Parménie. The hermitage where I would find Father de La Salle was very near and Jauffret did not want in any way to interfere with my mission. We embraced and he set out alone on his way to Grenoble. I watched him wave to me one last time in the distance.

My mission was about to end. The letter from the Brothers in Paris, ordering our superior to return, was safely hidden in the inner pocket of my coat. I felt both confident and anxious as I started up the steep slope of Parménie. In what state of mind and heart would I find Father de La Salle? Could I convey to him the love the Brothers had for him and the trust we placed in him? Could I convince him to return to Paris and take up the leadership of the Society, now almost on the verge of ruin? Was he well enough to do it? At this thought, the sorrow that I had felt so often during my journey swept over me again.

20

THE NARROW ROCKY path that I was following wound past a small flock of sheep clinging, I thought impossibly, onto that mountain side, then lost itself in the trees and shrubbery hiding the summit.

I had been climbing for an hour. The hamlets spotting the Isère valley through which I had passed hours ago lay silently far below. The giant Alps rose too far in the East to dwarf Parménie and the precipices of the Vercors to the South severed every remembrance of Grenoble except the sorrow that had seized me on learning that Father de La Salle had been so sick there and had come to this mountain retreat to rest—perhaps to stay for the rest of his life.

I climbed on until I reached a bubbling spring almost hidden by the mossy roots of a towering chestnut tree. Its message rang out crystal clear in the silent woods. The cool drink refreshed me and helped chase the fatigue from my tired limbs. For a moment I thought I heard the chatter of children coming up from the village below and my mind wandered back to the school on Princess Street and to the slums in Paris where I had grown up. But the sound died away and silence settled on the forest once more.

The path led on, steeper yet, to a very elevated point where I stopped once more to rest. The morning sun was high now and pleasantly warm. The horizon to the east, broken by the majestic Alps, gave me a sensation of peace and well being.

And then I saw it. Nestled in a clearing between two high grassy slopes were several small buildings of simple harmonious proportions, a miniature cloister, and a chapel whose picturesque bell tower stood out magnificently against the green of the forest, piercing the clear blue of the mountain sky.

As I approached, a young lad came running out into the clearing in front of the chapel.

"Hello," he said familiarly. "You are welcome here. I'm André. I help Sister Louise. Did you come far?"

"Quite far. From Paris. Is that far enough?"

"We have someone else here from Paris. Do you know him?"

"Yes, I think I do. Is it Father de La Salle? Where is he?"

"Oh, he is away today at Father de Saléon's place, down the hill. I hope he'll be back this evening or tomorrow. Will you stay with us?"

"Yes, if I may, but for a very short time. Until he comes."

"Why only a very short time? Father de La Salle wants to stay forever. He likes it here. He told me so."

"Maybe that is not possible. My name is Brother François. Tell me, is the Father Prior here?"

"This is no longer a monastery. The last monks left many years ago. Sister Louise restored the buildings and now she takes care of those who come here to pray. She is a saint."

"Why do you say that?"

"Because she is, that's all. God doesn't refuse her anything. You will see. Come along with me."

André led the way through the courtyard into a small cloister which was indeed charming and perfectly quiet. I was amused at hearing my own footsteps resound in the hollow vaulted archways. I stopped in order to listen to the dripping of the water in the well and the chirping of a bird. The sounds seemed to take on a particular charm, here within the silence of the cloister.

Intrigued by my reaction, and not wishing to break the silence, André led me to a corner where he insisted I remain, with my ear close to the wall. Then he ran playfully to the opposite corner and whispered to the wall, "Ave Maria."

The archway carried the echo in ripples over the stone, "Aveeee Mariaaaa."

The invocation came down to me in a tiny whisper and I had to smile as I answered, "Gratia plena."

I saw the boy catch the echo, "Gratiaaaa plenaaaa."
We both laughed.

André came from his corner and pointed up to a gargoyle near the roof. Adventurous swallows had made their home in its mouth, merrily fluttering in and out.

"Come, I'll show you where Father de La Salle stays when he is here. Perhaps he has come back by now. I go there often. He is teaching me how to read, but I am sometimes afraid that he'll go away for good some day before I learn."

I followed him up the stairs to a small room above the cloister. The door was open, the room empty. A large crucifix hung on one wall above a rustic prie-dieu. A small table, a chair, and a cot were all the furnishings. Nothing showed that the room had been occupied.

Lingering at the window, hoping that I might see him coming up the path, I thought of the message still hidden in my pocket and of the long dangerous journey I had made to deliver it to him personally.

"Why don't you come and meet Sister Louise? She'll tell you what you have to do."

"Who told you that I had to do something, André?"

The lad answered innocently, "My grandfather. He always used to say, `Believe me, André, those who come to this mountain come because they have a reason.' How did he put it? Something they must do. You should go and see her."

André led the way down the stairs and through the cloister to a room at the back of the hermitage.

From the door, I could see this woman whom everyone called Sister Louise. She was advanced in age, somewhat venerable looking, inspiring kindness. Her dress was plain and coarse. Everything about her, even her gestures, suggested the simplicity of country folk. In the room with her were three men, a woman, and a child, all poorly dressed sitting around a bare wooden table. One of the men had not removed his wide-brimmed hat.

"Sister Louise, this is Brother François." André said. "He has come all the way from Paris looking for Father de La Salle."

She came to the door.

"You are welcome, Brother. I have been thinking that someone would come for him," she said with straight forward simplicity. "God wants him to go back to Paris, I am quite sure, but I have been unable to convince him myself. Then, too, he has been ill. Come and sit down. You must be very tired and hungry. Our meal is simple, but with a little imagination you can turn it into a banquet."

Sister Louise welcomes Brother François to Parménie.

I took the place she showed me, noticing that everyone around the table was smiling. Sister Louise used a wooden ladle to fill our earthenware bowls with soup she had taken from the hearth.

After our meal, André took me to the highest point on the mountain, where a large cross had been planted in the rocky soil. From this vantage point, we could contemplate the breathtaking panorama that spread out before us on all sides. To the east, at the foot of the Alps, lay the Chartreuse Mountains.

André tugged at my arm, pointing out more than thirty villages, each with its church tower, dotting the plains far below. He knew them all by name. Then the clouds swept in and hid everything from view, leaving only the summit of Parménie, where we were standing in a strange, mysterious isolation, catching the last rays of the setting sun as it sank into that vast sea of white, staining it with red and gold.

The next morning I awoke to the sound of swallows outside my window, already busy about their day's adventure. André told me he would go down to the village to see his family and would stop at the Malines where Father de Saléon lived and tell Father de La Salle that I had arrived.

Sister Louise was at the well, lowering the wooden bucket. As she was about to draw it out, she saw me entering the cloister.

"I'm not sure your superior will listen to you. He has been with us for several months now, replacing Father de Saléon as chaplain. All he wants is privacy and peace to be alone with God and completely forgotten by the world."

"It is most important that I speak to him. The Brothers are very concerned about his health. How is he?"

"Much better, thank God. But he is a stubborn man." Then she paused and said simply, "I'm sorry, I shouldn't have said that. I tried to get him to return to Grenoble to the Brothers. There are doctors there. But he would not." She looked for a moment into the well. "I told him that it was God who made him the father of a very important family. He should not forget it. How he must have laughed at me. I'm not educated, you know. I can't read or write. Little André is more learned than I."

She prepared to draw up the bucket but I moved to take the rope.

"Let me help you. You must be very tired, with all this work."

She laughed very naturally and prevented me.

"As old as I am . . . That's really what you meant to say." She was pulling on the rope as she talked. "Here in the mountains, people don't get tired so easily." She drew the bucket out and emptied it in the curbstone of the well and caught her breath again. "Then, too, we never know just when we're tired enough to stop. No, we never know when we've reached the limit."

"All these people who visit Parménie, that must make you very happy," I said.

"Oh, they don't come on account of me."

"But, after all, you did restore the chapel and the buildings. They are grateful that you gave them back this beautiful place of prayer."

Sister Louise broke out laughing with so natural and genuine an air of surprise that I was taken aback.

"I was in prison," she said quickly.

I was dumbfounded.

"In prison?" I asked seriously.

"The Archbishop of Lyons put me there. Oh, but it's easy to understand. People told him there was an old lady in his diocese begging for alms for a convent in the South. It was for the buildings you see here. And the people were giving a lot, you know."

"Were you there a long time?"

"Oh, there were those who wanted to get me out right away. I told them no, no. Let me alone. It'll be when God wants. And you see, God took care of it in such a way that it was the same Archbishop himself who afterwards gave me more than all the others put together. That's why I always say we have to stay where we are."

"I suppose that is what you tell all these pilgrims."

"For sure! That's what I keep telling them. You'd think they came only to hear that, and they always seem to go away happy. Except your superior, that is. He is deeply troubled. I told him that too, but he thinks the Brothers have rejected him, that he is no longer capable of governing the teachers."

"But you surely know that that is not true. We love him dearly. We want him to come back. He must come back."

"Yes, I know. I showed him that pretty flower of the Alps they call Edelweiss. I wanted to plant it in my garden here but it wouldn't grow. God didn't make it to be pampered in a garden. It must be way up there on the highest peaks in the wind and snow where it can brave the fiercest blizzards. And so I told him that in seeking solitude he might not be doing the will of God, who surely did not want him to abandon the spiritual family he had given him."

I was deeply moved by the wisdom of this simple yet extraordinary woman. I felt a deep admiration and respect for her.

She stopped speaking as she rose, setting the bucket on the rim of the well. Looking off into the distance, as if inspired, she said: "Something is going to happen. Providence will give him the sign he is praying for. I am sure of it."

"We continued to sit quietly. Then she raised her hand, pointing and said:

"I think he has come back. Look, there on the path, near the cross. Why don't you go to him?"

"At last, at long last. Thank God."

I hurried up the slope.

We embraced for a long moment.

"Now, Brother François, tell me. What has happened? Why have you come?"

"Our community in Paris is in serious trouble. The ecclesiastical superiors want to revise the rules of the Society."

He looked pained.

"They say if we resist any of their changes, they will dissolve the group. The very existence of the Society is at stake. We need your leadership, Father. Come back to us. Only you can help us now."

"I can't." He spoke in a level tone just above a whisper. "I must not go back, for your own good." He waited a moment. "Can't you see that all the jealousy, the criticism, and the lawsuits have been aimed at me personally, not at the Brothers. I have only been an obstacle. The Brothers must learn to get along without me." He stopped. "Come, let us go inside. A storm is approaching."

I followed him down the path and into the cloister. Sister Louise had disappeared. We climbed the stairs to his room where he stood silent for a few moments before turning again to me, his aging but serene figure silhouetted against the window where thunder rumbled in the distance.

"We came in just in time," he said. "The storm is in the Alps now."

"How wonderful it feels to be safe here! Everything is so peaceful at Parménie."

"Yes, one hardly dares enjoy it."

"For fear that it will not last very long?" I asked.

Father de La Salle looked at me calmly, a question in his eyes.

"This is for you," I said, taking the envelope from my pocket.

"What is it?"

"A message from the Brothers, an appeal they have signed asking you to return."

He did not speak for a few moments. Then . . .

"I'm tired," he whispered. I continued to hold the envelope in my outstretched hand. His voice betrayed a certain emotion when he said, "Then read it, if you must."

I hesitated, my fingers trembling as I opened the envelope. It wasn't just a matter of reading the message. I knew it by heart, having recited it to myself over and over during the journey. It was the uncomfortable situation in which I found myself. I would have done anything in the world at that moment for Father de La Salle except ask him to leave this beautiful spot. Something besides the tone of his voice and his extraordinary calm urged me to get on with my task as bravely and as simply as I could.

He had gone to the window and was gazing outside. The whole atmosphere was one of utmost solemnity. Several doves had flown to the windowsill in front of him as if seeking refuge from the approaching storm. Down below, the serenity of the cloister contrasted vividly with the distant rumbling in the clouds and the claps of thunder. The water dripping into the well from the bucket hanging there echoed back. There above, in the mouth of the gargoyle, was the nest. It was empty. The swallows had gone.

I began to read:

Monsieur de La Salle, our very dear Father:

We the principal Brothers of the Christian Schools, having in view the greater glory of God as well as the good of the Church and of our Society, consider that it is of the greatest importance that you return to Paris and take up again the general direction of God's holy work, which is also your own, because it has pleased him to make use of you to establish it and guide it for so many years.

We are all convinced that God himself has called you to this work and that he has given you the grace and talents necessary for the good government of this new Society which is so beneficial to the Church. We acknowledge in all justice that you have always guided it with great success and edification. That is why, Monsieur de La Salle, we beseech you very humbly, and we order you in the name of the Society to which you have vowed obedience, to take up once more your duties as Superior of that Society.

In faith of which we have signed. Done in Paris, on this first day of April, 1714.

I folded the letter and placed it on the table. Father de La Salle remained near the window, motionless, his back to me.

I left the room. I could hear the storm as it broke over the monastery, heavy rain pouring down relentlessly.

The following day, we walked together up to the cross on the mountain top. The storm was over. Father de La Salle broke the long silence that had fallen between us.

"I will go back, Brother François, because God wants it that way." He embraced me and we again fell silent.

"It will be hard to leave this beautiful spot. How strange that Providence led me here, all the way from Paris, to meet a simple shepherdess. She told me that the letter you brought was the sign of God's will for me. She gave me the impression that she knew all along what was going to happen. Brother Barthélemy was right in sending the letter. I feel that I must obey. After all, I have tried to teach the Brothers obedience. It is time for me to practice it myself."

"It was a daring thing for us to do, Father. We were all afraid to sign it, but there was no other way. You are still our superior. We all recognize that. You do not have to obey the Brothers."

"Oh, but yes, this was a sign of Providence and I have always tried to let Providence be my guide. Let me tell you this, Brother François, in all sincerity. If God, in showing me all the good that our Society would bring about in the world, had also revealed to me all the pain and sorrow that I would have to go through to establish it, my courage would have faltered and I would not have dared to touch it, not even with the tip of my fingers."

We stopped only a few yards from the cross. "But God conducts all things with wisdom and kindness, and never forces our will. God got me interested in taking complete control of the schools and led me imperceptibly, over a long period of time, to make one commitment after another without my being aware of how involved I would eventually become. If I had known at the beginning that the interest I had taken in Monsieur Nyel's school teachers, through pure charity, would have led me to share my life with them under the same roof, I would have abandoned the project altogether.

"You see, Brother François, it is all God's work, really, and God will see it through. Shall we go back to the hermitage now and make ready for our departure?"

André was running up the hill toward us.

"I brought these for you both. I gathered them in the forest." He held out his hands, full of chestnuts. Then, looking up into the priest's face, he said, "You seem so different today, Father de La Salle. Sister Louise told me you are going away. Are you happy to go away? I thought you liked it here."

"Thank you, André. Thank you very much. O yes, I like it here. I would stay forever, if I could, but I have to go back to the Brothers in Paris. They are my family, just as Sister Louise said."

"If she told you to do that, it must be right." André paused a moment, then said hesitatingly "Did Sister Louise tell you that someone is waiting to see you at the monastery?

"No. Is there someone?"

"A Monsieur Dulac. He is an officer in the King's army but he's not dressed like a soldier now. He was wounded in battle. Father de Saléon told me about him. He's a hero."

"Now what can this be about?" Father de La Salle sighed.

As André led us down the hill to the hermitage, a tall young man came out of the chapel. He was distinguished looking, though dressed in very rough peasant clothes.

"Father de La Salle?" he questioned.

"Yes, and this is Brother François."

"I've been wanting to meet you. I'm Claude Dulac de Montisambert. You will excuse such familiarity, I hope, but when God prompts us . . . "

"God whispers in your ear like that? You are very lucky."

Father de La Salle smiled.

"For almost a year, I have been going from one monastery to another, all the way to Rome and back, but no one will have me. The monks are afraid of my father, perhaps. He doesn't want me to give up my military career and enter a monastery. He has even sent out a search warrant to bring me back."

"And what are you asking of me?"

"I used to have the title of lieutenant in the King's army, but I was just a lightheaded fool. I squandered much of my father's fortune over the card table and led a frivolous life. I want to enter the Society of teachers that you have founded, if you will have me. Father de Saléon must have spoken to you."

"Let's wait to talk further," Father de La Salle said. "After dinner we will have time."

"Of course, but please don't deprive me of the hope that some day I will be called Brother."

"Brother Claude?"

"No, not that. I am anxious to bid farewell to Claude."

"What then?"

"You'll find a good name for me."

"We shall see."

Later that evening I learned that Father de La Salle had indeed heard many good things about Claude Dulac from Father de Saléon. Aside from his pilgrimages, the young man had spent many months in Grenoble, living very simply, caring for the poor and the sick in the public hospital and attending daily religious services. He seemed very determined to follow a religious vocation despite the opposition of his father. Sister Louise, who had recently come to know him, assured Father de La Salle in a kind of prophetic way that Dulac was destined to become one of the most important members of our Society.

Following these strong recommendations, Father de La Salle interviewed the young man several times the next few days in order to test his virtue and his determination. He finally decided to receive Dulac into the Society. He gave him the name Brother Irénée, in memory of Saint Irenaeus, a Bishop who had been martyred for his faith very near Parménie in the early days of the Church. The identity of Claude Dulac de Montisambert and the story of his extraordinary vocation were to be kept secret so that he might escape from any opposition on the part of his father.

I could see clearly that Father de La Salle's leadership and his confidence for the future of our Society were stirred and strengthened by his encounter with Claude Dulac. We stayed on at Parménie for several more days to get better acquainted with him and were edified by the joy and fervor with which he made his retreat.

Brother Jacques, the director of the school in Grenoble, came to Parménie to bid us farewell and to take the new Brother back to the city with him. Dulac would receive the Brother's robe there and then begin his new career as a teacher.

The morning that Father de La Salle had set for our departure dawned bright and clear. Sister Louise sent André for a small horse-drawn cart and driver to take us down the mountain to the main road. She kissed Father de La Salle's hand and asked his blessing. We both hugged André.

As we drove slowly away, down the slope, André came running playfully behind the cart.

"Ave Maria," I called out.

The lad stopped and called back, "Gratia plena."

We watched him standing there waving, until his little figure disappeared in the sky above the hermitage.

21

WE RODE ON, Father de La Salle and I, two lone figures on horseback, along the route to Paris. Parménie was now far behind us, but not at all forgotten.

We rode on to Lyons to pray at the tomb of Saint Francis de Sales, a saint who had made himself very dear to the people in this part of France. In Dijon, we made another stop, staying with the Brothers for several days and bringing them the good news of the schools in the South.

We rode on now to Versailles, skirting its immense park and gardens, its fountains and magnificent palace. The reception given us here, in the poorest part of the town, at the simple dwelling of the Brothers, touched our hearts. I thought of other receptions, those given in this very city by Louis XIV, whom his admirers called the Sun King—receptions for poets, musicians, architects, generals, orators, cardinals—the greatest geniuses that France had ever known. I thought, too, of Julien Clément and of Nicolas Vuyart, dressed in their courtly attire, and of a drawing room in Reims where someone was playing the harpsichord.

We rode on, nearer and nearer our journey's end, and into Paris at last. All along the way I had noticed the vitality returning to Father de La Salle. And now as we came through the streets of Paris, I knew he had regained his full spirit and confidence. We approached the community on La Barouillère Street.

It was a homecoming for Father de La Salle, and we all rejoiced. The care and attention the Brothers had not been able to show him during his absence were now lavished on him in abundance. In quiet, prayerful joy he returned their affection, and during the weeks that followed he gave all his time to visiting the schools in and near Paris, interviewing each of the Brothers, encouraging them in their work, and spreading the good news of the foundations in the provinces.

In Paris, peace reigned once more for our Society. The storms that were raging so furiously at the time of my departure had calmed. Father de La Chétardye had died during my absence and the cardinal had not approved Monsieur de Brou's attempt to modify the rules of our Society. Soon after Monsieur Clément and his son had won the case against Father de La Salle, the young cleric, Abbot of Saint-Calais, had fallen into disgrace at Court. The civil authorities were glad to forget his accusations against Father de La Salle. The fragile bark that was our Society had weathered the storm; the skies were clearing and the waters subsiding.

After spending several months in Paris, Father de La Salle moved the novitiate to Saint Yon in Rouen. He hoped to pass the remaining years of his life there. Brother Barthélemy was sent on a long journey to visit every community in order to prepare the Brothers for a general meeting at which elections would be held to name one of the Brothers as superior of the Society.

The work in Rouen had developed considerably. At Saint Yon, besides the novitiate, a boarding school and a house of correction were also functioning. Brother Antoine had been given charge of this latter institution and he had proved himself a competent superior. Under his care were a good number of unruly individuals whom the state had confided to the custody of the Brothers. It would have disgraced the families of the offenders to condemn these young criminals to serve time in public prisons. Through Father de La Salle's influence many of these wayward youths were converted to better lives.

Brother Antoine told me of one particularly curious case. A young man had come to Saint Yon some months ago from another school in the city, where he was not wanted because of his misconduct and disregard for all authority. He took a liking to Father de La Salle at once and the two could often be seen talking together. The change that came over the young renegade was unbelievable. Before very long he had not only been promoted from the house of correction to the boarding school, but he was actually taking part in some of the activities of the novitiate. Soon he asked to become a Brother. The boy's parents considered his joining the Brothers below their dignity and would not give their consent, though they expressed great delight at the startling change in their son's conduct. The young man kept writing for the desired permission until finally the parents stopped answering his letters altogether. Taking this as a sign of their consent, Father de La Salle gave him the habit of the Brothers and allowed him to begin his novitiate.

Some months later a coach drew up before the front gate of the school. Two gentlemen alighted and asked to see the new novice. No sooner had he appeared than they snatched him up by force, hurried him into the coach and signaled the driver to be off as fast as the horses could run. That was the last anyone ever saw of Father de La Salle's young convert, but a letter arrived some time later from his grief-stricken and repentant parents saying that their son had not been happy since they had taken him away from the novitiate. He had died soon after, asking for the robe he had worn for so brief a period.

When Brother Barthélemy returned from his mission, Father de La Salle convoked the assembly that was to elect his successor. During the retreat that preceded the election, our superior spoke to us very eloquently of our mission as educators. Feeling that this might, perhaps, be our last time together with him, we considered his words as a testament to be guarded preciously.

"By your profession, you are real apostles," he said, "apostles who share in the ministry that Christ confided to his Church. Your employment, your very mission in life, obliges you to touch hearts. You cannot do so without the Spirit of God. Pray to him often that he grant you the same grace he gave to the Apostles so that when you are sanctified through his Spirit, you may communicate that Spirit to your pupils for their salvation."

We listened attentively, knowing that it was not as some talented pedagogue that he spoke to us. The remarkable educational reforms that he had brought about during the last thirty years had been inspired by Father de La Salle's extraordinary faith and zeal. "Do not distinguish," he told us, "between the things you do for your own growth and deepening of faith and the things you do to prepare and teach class. Let everything be done for God and as an expression of God's love."

We were proud of what Father de La Salle had done for us, of what he had done for the artisans and the poor, of what he had done for the Church. Our schools were not only places of learning, they were places where the poor could hear and share the good news of the gospel. We were proud to be his disciples, now numbering more than a hundred, teaching in twenty-six schools throughout France. There was also the school in Rome where Brother Gabriel Drolin had remained faithful to the mission Father de La Salle had confided to him fifteen years ago.

In the election that followed this retreat, Brother Barthélemy received the majority of votes. This was not a surprise. Father de La Salle had prepared both him and the Brothers for this election and was the first to congratulate him, to kneel at his feet and kiss his hand as a sign of obedience. The new superior and all the Brothers present were deeply moved at seeing the Founder of the Society in that humble position.

From that day on, no one in the house seemed quite as happy as Father de La Salle, and certainly no one excelled him in obedience and submission to the newly elected superior.

Brother Barthélemy was loved by all of us. During Father de La Salle's absence from Paris, he had already proved himself a kind father to all the Brothers and now that the full responsibility of superiorship had been placed on his shoulders, he became all the more devoted to the general welfare of the Society.

As the first months of 1719 passed by, we saw less and less of Father de La Salle. Despite his rheumatism and other ailments, he chose to live in a tiny room at the back of the house and there spent much of his time either in prayer or in revising the books that he had written, seemingly undisturbed by the noise of the children playing in the schoolyard below his window. These books were the result of his many years of experience working with just such children. Father de La Salle's writings were a kind of last will and testament, a culmination of all his faith and work, his love and care. They suggested many practical measures to succeed in the classroom and inspired us with his vision in carrying out our mission.

By the middle of March, Father de La Salle's health had declined so rapidly that the doctors no longer hoped for any kind of recovery. On the feast of Saint Joseph, March 19, he surprised everyone by rising from his bed to celebrate the Eucharist with all the Brothers of the community. He looked so well that some of us thought there had been a miracle, that our prayers had been answered. In early April, however, his state became more alarming than ever; and yet, all those who visited him left the sick room deeply edified by the calm, indefinable happiness that radiated from his person.

One evening we were all gathered in his room to say the rosary with him. He was sitting up in an armchair and seemed extremely exhausted. After the prayers, he looked up, as if speaking to someone we could not see, and said "Why so soon?"

No one understood what he meant. I went nearer and questioned him. "What do you mean, Father? Why so soon?"

"There is so much yet to do and I have done so little," he said. "I have dreamed of schools for the poor all over the world, and of teachers—hundreds of them."

He looked at us. "Remain as united as you are now. God will bless you and his kingdom will come."

Brother Antoine and I helped him back into bed, but even when he was again lying down he seemed restless.

"Why are you all here like this?" he said. "Is someone taking care of the boys in the yard? I don't hear them. Isn't it recreation time."

"We asked them to be quiet today so as not to disturb you," Brother Barthélemy said.

"Let them play as usual. I like to hear them."

Brother Antoine went to the window and made a sign to the youngsters gathered in the yard. At once they began to play and to shout merrily.

"That is much better. Thank you, Brother Antoine. I always go to the window at this hour. I want to see them. I want them to see me."

The effort to rise was too great for him and he fell back exhausted onto his pillow. He closed his eyes and remained motionless for a long while. One after another, we slipped quietly from the room. Only Brother Barthélemy kept vigil near the bedside.

It was just at this time, when Father de La Salle was very near death, that there occurred yet another of those misunderstandings with the ecclesiastical authorities which had been such a marked feature of his life. The pastor of Saint Sever parish where Saint Yon was located complained that we were not taking our boarding students to Mass in the parish church on Sundays. He accused Father de La Salle of not keeping his promise. It is true that at one time, we had made such an agreement with the pastor, but now that many of the boarding students were delinquents, confided to us by the courts, we could no longer take them into the streets for fear that some of them might escape.

The disgruntled pastor took the matter to the Archbishop, Mgr. d'Aubigné, who not only lent a willing ear to the complaints but decided to deprive Father de La Salle of the right to say Mass or hear confessions as chaplain of the Brothers' community. Though this news must have hurt him deeply, he showed no exterior signs of losing his peace of soul.

On Holy Thursday evening, we gathered again in his room when Holy Communion was brought to him for the last time. After the prayers of thanksgiving, Brother Barthélemy asked Father de La Salle to give us his blessing. Raising his eyes to heaven and lifting his hands, he made a sign of the cross and said very slowly, "May the good God, Father, Son and Holy Spirit, bless all of you."

His hands fell back on his breast, clinging to his crucifix. His eyes closed. He was losing consciousness.

Toward midnight, he recovered slightly and began to recite the prayer to our Blessed Lady which we always said together at night.

> Mary, Mother of grace,
> Sweet Mother of mercy,
> Defend us from the enemy,
> And receive us at the hour of death.

A long, prayerful silence followed. We were all still kneeling around his bed when his last words came to us, slowly but very clearly, like an echo of his whole life: "I adore in all things the will of God in my regard." Then, very calmly, he made an effort to rise, as if he desired to go forward to meet someone.

The peaceful smile that lingered on his lips, even after death, spoke eloquently of the glorious rendezvous he kept with his Lord that Good Friday morning, April 7, 1719.

De La Salle dies in Rouen on Good Friday, April 7, 1719.

Epilogue

MANY YEARS PASSED before I went back to Parménie, where in 1714 I had found Father de La Salle.

I prayed at the tomb of Sister Louise. To me, she seemed rather to be standing there by the well in the cloister. I remembered little André. Pilgrims told me that after the death of Sister Louise, he had gone off to Avignon to join the Brothers. I thought, too, of Lieutenant Claude du Lac de Montisambert. He had indeed become Brother Irénée and was now the director of novices at Saint Yon. Sister Louise's prophecy about him had come true.

I entered the tiny rustic chapel, its bare rock walls more beautiful and eloquent than ever before. Multicolored light poured in from the stained glass windows, a soft, penetrating light, like that in the cathedral of Reims. It gave the sanctuary a sort of sacred intimacy. I knelt on the very spot where Father de La Salle used to say his Mass. In those few moments of prayer, I realized in the depth of my being what had really happened here and I thanked the Lord, my heart full of happiness and peace.

Outside, in the welcoming shade of the forest, the nightingales were singing. I followed the narrow grassy path where he used to walk with a prayer book in his hands. I reached the cross near the top of the mountain, the place where we had embraced that morning years ago when he had said very simply, "I'll go back, Brother François, because God wants it that way." I could see him again walking slowly down toward the chapel. On the wings of the wind his message came back to me:

Real wealth consists in being free,
in not being possessed by possessions,
in sharing and in loving.
Children know this.
There is no class distinction among them.
If I can open their minds and let the sun enter in,
if enough of us can do this,
if we can lead them beyond the boundaries that enslave them,
then the world will become a brighter place,
and people will live closer to justice,
closer to happiness
and closer
to peace.

About the Author

 BROTHER LEO BURKHARD, a Coloradoan by birth, joined the Christian Brothers in 1939 and has since taught in the United States, in Mexico, in France and in Italy. He holds a doctorate in history from the University of Grenoble, France. Much of the time he spent abroad was devoted to historical research about a small mountain in southern France named Parménie and to the restoration of an ancient monastery there which has since become the Brothers novitiate for the French Region. His writings, whether in French, English or Spanish, center mostly around this extraordinary spot where he lived for twenty-five years and its connection with De La Salle, the founder of the Christian Brothers. In recognition of Brother Leo's work there, the French government awarded him the National Order of Merit in 1990.

Beyond the Boundaries is Brother Leo's latest work. His other books include: *Master of Mischief Makers* (1952); *Un Gamin de Paris* (1959); *Parménie, Haut Lieu Dauphinois* (1964); *L'Etonnante et Fascinante Histoire d'une Petite Colline Dauphinoise* (1976); *Encounters: De La Salle at Parménie* (1983); *Un Pilluelo de Paris Encuentra al Señor de La Salle* (1985); *Parménie et la Crise de Jean-Baptiste de La Salle et de son Institut de 1712–1714* (Cahier Lasallien No. 57) (1994).

Endorsements

Reading this book brought me to know and love De La Salle, the Founder of the Brothers. I got so involved as I read further and further into the story, that I actually felt like one of the characters, if not the story teller himself. . . . A truly unique experience.

Luis Alberto Munoz, FSC
Christian Brothers Novitiate, Mexico

The succession of dramatic scenes in *Beyond the Boundaries* carries the reader along and excites eager expectations. I was amazed at the amount of authentic historical and biographical background woven into the book. People and events come to life.

Brother Richard Segura, FSC, PhD
Professor Emeritus of English, College of Santa Fe